BEST RADIO
PLAYS OF 1989

BEST RADIO PLAYS OF 1989

with an Introduction
by Frances Gray

The Giles Cooper Award Winners

Elizabeth Baines: The Baby Buggy
Jennifer Johnston: O Ananias, Azarias and Misael
David Zane Mairowitz: The Stalin Sonata
Richard Nelson: Eating Words
Craig Warner: By Where the Old Shed Used to Be

METHUEN/BBC PUBLICATIONS

First published in Great Britain in 1990 by Methuen Drama,
Michelin House, 81 Fulham Road, London SW3 6RB and in the
USA by HEB Inc, 70 Court Street, Portsmouth, New Hampshire
03801 and BBC Publications, 35 Marylebone High Street,
London W1M 4AA.

A CIP catalogue record for this book
is available from the British Library

ISBN 0-413-63240-7

Typeset in Garamond by
Hewer Text Composition Services, Edinburgh
Printed in Great Britain by
St Edmundsbury Press, Bury St Edmunds, Suffolk

CONTENTS

THE GILES COOPER AWARDS: a note on the selection

Giles Cooper

As one of the most original and inventive radio playwrights of the post-war years, Giles Cooper was the author who came most clearly to mind when the BBC and Methuen were in search of a name when first setting up their jointly sponsored radio drama awards in 1978. Particularly so, as the aim of the awards is precisely to encourage original radio writing by both new and established authors – encouragement in the form of both public acclaim and of publication of their work in book form.

Eligibility

Eligible for the awards was every original radio play first broadcast by the BBC domestic service from December 1988 to December 1989 (almost 500 plays in total). Excluded from consideration were translations, adaptations and dramatised 'features'. In order to ensure that the broad range of radio playwriting was represented, the judges aimed to select plays which offered a variety of length, subject matter and technique by authors with differing experience of writing for radio.

Selection

The editors-in-charge and producers of the various drama 'slots' were each asked to put forward about five or six plays for the judges' consideration. This resulted in a 'short-list' of some 30 plays from which the final selection was made. The judges were entitled to nominate further plays for consideration provided they were eligible. Selection was made on the strength of the script rather than of the production, since it was felt that the awards were primarily for writing and that production could unduly enhance or detract from the merits of the original script.

Judges

The judges for the 1989 awards were:
  Pamela Edwardes, Drama Editor, Methuen Drama
  Penny Gold, Senior Editor of BBC Radio Drama
  Rob Ritchie, a writer and former literary manager of the Royal Court Theatre, London
  B. A. Young, radio drama critic for the *Financial Times*

INTRODUCTION

Compare two party games. In Kim's Game you are shown a tray of small objects – paperclips and so on – for thirty seconds. Then it's removed and you have to remember them. In Chinese Whispers a message is whispered down a line of people and becomes transformed in the process. The assumptions behind these games say a good deal about our attitudes to the senses. Kim's Game is about skill; it's competitive. You can teach the brain to recall accurately what the eye saw and the best players will remember everything. The less skilful will forget a few objects but, by and large, they won't recall things not actually there in the first place. In Chinese Whispers, however, the untrustworthiness of the ear is the whole point. A simple message, 'My name is Martin Harold West', is sloppily hissed down the line. The ear picks up a jumble of vowels and consonants – but our instinct is not to accept meaningless jumbles; rather we attempt to make sense of them by bringing the imagination into play. The brain understands the way our language is constructed; the imagination uses that knowledge to fill in the inaudible gaps with something intelligible and comes up with a statement perhaps more poetically resonant than the original: 'Adam farted in the wild forest.' This is, essentially, a cooperative game, with complex interplay between speaker, listener and the imagination, and as such it has an admirable potential for developing party relationships. No one, on the other hand, ever flirted over a tray of paperclips.

This interplay between the ear and the imagination doesn't just operate in terms of words. Stand in a familiar place and close your eyes. At once, the world changes. You are in the grounds of a hospital, but what you hear is a child laughing. You are in the heart of an industrial city, but what you hear is birdsong. New pictures form in your head, with new connotations, and the city and the hospital will never look the same again. The ear has been disconcerted. Our imagination operates certain codes or conventions. In a hospital setting you expect ambulance sirens: think of the sounds of a city, and you think of traffic. But, however accustomed it is to such codes, the ear can always relish a surprise, a chance to re-evaluate them.

The radio playwright's task is to exploit this relationship between the sound, the ear and the imagination, to play on both our expectations and our uncertainties. A radio play, like a game of Chinese Whispers, is a cooperative act, and one involving a degree of intimacy on the part of the players. Words and sounds set us creating a picture in our minds. The writer gives us a cue with a line like, 'How beautiful the sea looks today', but we are then free to develop the details of the imagined landscape for ourselves. However, cooperation isn't always as simple as it seems. Suppose the remark about the sea is followed by a brisk voice saying, 'You're hallucinating again, it's time for your injection.' Our mental landscape will be rapidly replaced – but, nevertheless, we shared the 'hallucination' with the first speaker and our perspective on the new scene will be affected by this. And if the next sound is a clipped military voice announcing the neccessity to keep political prisoner K constantly sedated, the ear and the imagination have to go to work again . . .

This power of existential flexibility gives the radio playwright an opportunity virtually unique in the dramatic media; it is often said that the true stage of radio is the mind, but it might be more accurate to characterise the mind as a theatre, a place in which a new 'stage' is created by, and for, each play. If we consider exactly what a stage is and does, the value of the playwright's opportunity becomes quickly apparent. Basically, a stage comprises a set of signs, a code between the creators of the play and the audience. Its shape will be determined by a cultural consensus about the nature of reality. The Middle Ages, for instance, believed in a world with a tangible heaven above the clouds and a fiery hell beneath the earth, and constructed a three decker stage for the Miracle plays as the agreed code for it. The nineteenth century – man- rather than God-centred – created a brightly lit box containing a physically accurate reproduction of the less private living spaces of the dominant class, on which actors showed 'live' lived upon highly specific ideological assumptions. The world of Beckett's *Not I* contains only one certainty, the fact that someone is speaking, and the total darkness surrounding the endlessly moving mouth is the spatial code by which we understand this. These spatial codes will in turn affect the relationship between audience and actor. The onstage Victorian world wanted no dialogue with the audience about the assumptions it signified; the Miracle plays, about our own salvation, thrived on it; our relationship to Beckett's mouth is one of the questions *Not I* invites us to ponder: would it speak if we were not there?

Radio of course can only move in time, not in space. But if the play is to mean anything, the playwright must create the *illusion* of space, and by so doing must make clear the reality of the play's world. This created 'stage' can be a far more flexible and delicate instrument than the average theatre provides.

Take, for instance, the three plays in this volume which have some sort of relationship to the idea of 'naturalism', that is, to the apparently artless reproduction of our empirically observable world: *Eating Words*, *The Baby Buggy* and *O Ananias, Azarias and Misael*. Each develops a highly individual and complex relationship with the audience on its 'stage'. Richard Nelson opens *Eating Words* with a short announcement followed by some everyday-sounding dialogue – the kind of beginning, in fact, that we are familiar with in *The Archers*. For a time the play seems no more than a mercilessly accurate portrayal of two writers, Henry and Sam, their little vanities and their shameless exploitation of family and friends for new copy. There's a wickedly funny use of subtext:

> SAM. . . . The stories were just sitting there to incorporate.
> *Beat.*
> I observe life. This is what we do, Henry. That is how I see it.
> *Short pause.*
> And Ben's going to college next year. You can't afford to start getting picky.

But the play rapidly pushes out from the naturalistic frame to set their problems in the wider context of the writer's function in society. It acquires a surreal dimension: Henry and Sam are berated in a pub by a young woman in whom Thatcherism has reached a pitch of rhapsody so infectious that the normally stolid punters rabidly join in her game of Bait the Intellectual. The mock-heroic titles which preface each section move from simple scene-setting, to ironising Henry and Sam, to forcing us to ponder the questions they dream of illuminating in their own work – questions to which, ultimately, they may never be able to do justice, but for which they genuinely care. It is, in the end, despite its small scale, a political play.

The same could be said of Elizabeth Baines's *The Baby Buggy*. Again, the surface is apparently that of simple naturalism, with a few spoken thoughts, an account of a woman's early days of motherhood. But the focus of each scene – literally, a buggy – seems so obsessively narrow that it foregrounds itself; the narrowness forces us to realise that we are not watching an unbroken bit of surface life; we are hearing carefully selected fragments of a woman's experience – the only moments of sympathy she receives for the physical and mental stress she is encountering; it makes her talkative, and consequently these also become the only moments when she cannot pretend to ignore the gap that is opening up between her expectations of life for women in the eighties and the painful realities. Baines gives us few details of Di's life outside these inconsequential minutes with her friend, but she enables us to construct them – and judge the world which produces them – for ourselves.

We engage in this process, too, in Jennifer Johnston's *O Ananias, Azarias and Misael*: the 'stage' here is the simplest of all, that of the storyteller who addresses us directly. It suits the intimacy of radio perfectly. But we are not passive listeners. Johnston plants a wealth of detail to place Christine in context – political, social, sexual; as she tells us the story of her life Christine herself never dwells on these with anything like anger or resentment, although they are tragic details; but the telling of her story is clearly, for her, a necessary act, a way of saying goodbye to a life. Our relationship with her is thus dynamic; while we grow in awareness of the social forces that shape her we also develop increasing respect for her as an individual struggling with them.

In David Zane Mairowitz's *The Stalin Sonata*, the subject is radio and the stage created has a complex double nature. He opens in the world of black political farce; his media men construct the 'reality' of Stalinism according to precise rules – the new announcer on the music programme learns the prescribed vocal inflections for naming the artists whose records he plays: 'You must never assume that someone's status will be as it was last week. It may well have been changed from "exclamatory" to "monotone" . . .' When Stalin himself telephones to request a recording of a discredited pianist and she is dragged out of prison half-dead to cut a disc, the play retains this cartoon-like edge (bearing in mind that in the world of the dictator the cartoon can be more accurate than the photograph). But it also invites us to experience the action on a level denied the stage of political farces – that of speaking silence. The pianist, Maria Lvovna, is too ill to talk; occasionally she can communicate with ironic sharpness through the keyboard – witness her brilliantly radiophonic dialogue with her former lover and betrayer conducted entirely through popular tunes. But radio makes it possible for us to eavesdrop on her thoughts; through them we discover that while words like 'counter-revolutionary' have no fixed meaning, they can indicate lived and terrible experience. Lvovna's (impossible) articulated silences are literally the only way, in this world, that the reality of her experience can exist and be judged against the one created in the radio station.

Craig Warner's *By Where the Old Shed Used to Be* takes radio flexibility to extremes – realities breed like rabbits. Sometimes his world looks familiar: the heroine is the youngest of three daughters, her father's favourite, and when he dies her sisters are unkind to her, uttering satisfyingly baroque threats to rip out her vocal cords and use them for elasticating knickers. But then this Cinderella figure has a sophisticated line in revenge rather than saintly patience; there's a noble youth who loves her in lyrical prose, with a lager-swilling sidekick of baser instincts, but when the sidekick drags our hero off to a strip joint, it turns out that the girls reveal themselves *psychologically*. If you turn to the narrator to get your bearings, tough, because the lager-drinker shoots her, only to find that he can't control the story either. But with every jolt on this existential switchback we find ourselves asking questions about stories and siblings and sexuality and learn to take no more for granted than does the narrator herself.

Radio, then, can create any world, any reality. A playwright couldn't ask for more, really, in order to provoke thought. And given that it can do so for an audience of millions for the cost of a bit of tape, with a rehearsal period about a tenth of that of a reasonable rep, nor could an enterprise culture . . . except, as Henry and Sam discovered, that there are systems not a million miles from home more interested in money than provoking thought. The Ugly Vision in the Inn tells them, 'I'm in the real world, okay?' Perhaps radio's most important function at present is to render that point debatable.

Frances Gray, April 1990

THE BABY BUGGY

by Elizabeth Baines

Elizabeth Baines was born in South Wales in 1947 and studied English at the University College of North Wales, Bangor. She taught in Scotland for some years. She began writing while expecting her first child, at a time when having a baby still meant losing a teaching-post. She has published numerous short stories in literary and popular magazines and anthologies, and two novels, *The Birth Machine* (Women's Press) and *Body Cuts* (Pandora). Her first radio play was *Rhyme or Reason*, which was first broadcast in 1987, and for which Harriet Walter won a Sony Radio Best Actress award. *The Baby Buggy* is Elizabeth Baines's second radio play. She lives in Manchester with the writer John Ashbrook and her two sons.

The Baby Buggy was first broadcast on BBC Radio 4 as an 'Afternoon Play' on 16 August 1989. The cast was as follows:

DI   Linda Bassett
SANDY   Barbara Marten

Director: Susan Hogg
Running time, as broadcast: approximately 45 minutes

The present. Interior.

SANDY. I'd have given you my baby buggy –

DI. Oh no –

SANDY. I must say, Di, I never thought you –

DI. I know!

SANDY. I never thought you and Jim –

DI. *I* never thought –

SANDY. After all this time . . .

DI. Well, this was a mistake.

SANDY. Oh . . .!

DI. Honestly, the one and only time I ever forgot to put my cap
in –

SANDY. Oh . . .!

DI. And women of forty aren't meant to be that fertile!

SANDY. Oh dear . . .

DI. You're right, we were always so determined not to – and to go
and do it now, when everyone else like you has almost got it all
behind you . . .

SANDY. Oh dear . . .

Pause.

DI. Mind you . . . I mean, I'm not pretending it isn't a problem, but,
generally speaking, if you do have children later, it can be less of a
trap in a way. You've learnt to handle things, haven't you? You're
more mature . . . For God's sake we're old enough at least to be

philosophical . . . this was when we were discussing the idea of me having an abortion – well, it was an option we had to consider seriously – I said to him, 'You know, when you think about it, we don't actually need to panic like we might have fifteen years ago.' So . . . well, it's going ahead . . . This woman from work has given me a load of baby things . . .

SANDY. I'd have given you my buggy –

DI. Oh, no, Sandy, this woman has given me hers . . . she started back at work last September, after having her three kids . . . it's well-used, I guess, but perfectly functional, I mean, I don't need anything fancy – God, I'm too old after all for that kind of fuss!

Pause.

Jim said straight off, once it was decided: 'I'm not spending a fortune,' and he's absolutely right. There's just no point, is there? After all, they're babies for hardly any time, nothing gets used for very long. I guess that's another advantage; at least you know that, having seen your friends go through it before you – I mean, look at yours, at secondary school already! I won't go mad feeling it's going to go on for ever, the way I know you did. And that's another thing: we come in for all the hand-me-downs and save a whole load of expense . . . The buggy's one of those transportable ones, you fold it up . . .

SANDY. Oh, like mine was.

DI. Oh, was it? (*Pause.*) Yes, well, the collapsible kind.

Pause.

Do you remember the prams our mothers had?

SANDY. God, yes, like boats weren't they?

DI. Like barges.

SANDY. Like tanks.

DI. And just as awkward to manoeuvre.

SANDY. Too big to go anywhere.

DI. Too heavy.

SANDY. And enormous wheels that wouldn't go upstairs.

DI. Yes, women were stuck at the bottom with prams.

Pause.

Things do change, don't they? I mean, pram designs have had to change because women's expectations of their lives have changed . . .

Pause.

SANDY. I remember sitting in my pram.

DI. Good Lord, do you?

Background garden sounds. Interior monologue.

SANDY. I was parked in the garden under a tree. Now and then my
mother would pop out to check I was all right. The pram had a
canopy with a silky fringe. I kicked my legs, and when I did the pram
squeaked and the glistening fringe wriggled like snakes. Whenever
the pram squeaked my mother popped out her head. I kicked, and
she popped out her head. In my canopied throne, I had her in my
power. Later I vowed I would never get trapped like that.

Cut garden sounds.

DI. How can you remember so far back? I remember walking by the
side of my brother's pram.

*Fade up exterior. DI and her mother pushing the pram in the street
in heavy rain. Then dip under interior monologue.*

DI. I had no gloves on, and the handle of the pram was wet and steely
cold. My mother was bad-tempered, no wonder – she was pushing
against the rain and wind; the great white wheel went through a
puddle and splashed it up our legs. 'Stop whining,' she snapped. She
stopped and kicked the pram-brake on, so hard, taking it out on it,
the whole pram juddered, and my baby brother looked shocked.
'Stay there,' she said briskly – you couldn't take a pram anywhere.
'Don't let strangers stick their heads in.' She went inside the building,
gloomy-grey with metal plates on the doors. And I had to stay on
guard outside in the slinging icy rain.

*Fade up rain briefly to surreal proportions, then dip under following
interior monologue.*

Later I decided you'd never catch me trundling a pram and wet
whining kids through the rain.

Present. Interior.

DI. Well, we'd every reason to dread pregnancy then, hadn't we?
Remember what happened to you, remember how miserable it made
you?

Crossfade to flashback.

SANDY. 7th June 1973.

Dear Di,
You won't believe this. I'm pregnant. And just after landing the new
job as well! And needless to say they'll kick me straight out. I'll be
just a housewife after all . . .

Fade.

Present. Interior.

DI. Well, you hardly had a chance to see the positive aspects, did you? . . . I'm not being sentimental or anything, but it is a bit amazing isn't it, that thought of life being inside you . . . (*Abruptly.*) Well, thank goodness it's not like that now. Dreadful – I mean, you never did get back full-time, did you? How many talented women's careers have been destroyed in that way? Actually, at our place it's particularly good. I've got six months on full pay, and then of course I walk straight back and carry on where I left off. Things have changed a hell of a lot, haven't they? Women no longer need be plunged into isolation and dependency just because they've had a child.

Crossfade to flashback. (Possibly more distant acoustic?)

SANDY.
Dear Di,
I was so sorry not to meet you in London as I'd hoped, but with Dave working that weekend and the fact that we're not very well off for babysitters at the mo, it really would have been very difficult. Oh, I know how feeble that sounds, it's hard to convey how difficult it is sometimes; I guess half my problem is depression, but then it is also a fact that we can hardly afford babysitters. Babies are so expensive, I find it hard to believe myself that anyone so little could cost quite so much! And with only one salary coming in . . .

Cut in with present.

DI. As I say, that's one of the ironies, we've two top salaries, neither of them threatened, and yet doing it so much later we get everyone else's stuff and we're saved so much expense!

Continue flashback.

SANDY. Perhaps you could come down some weekend and stay as we do find it so hard to get away? Oh, it would be lovely to see you again after all this time – time might have flown to you, but it seems ages to me, and if I don't see people soon I might well strangle the little blighters, I'm afraid!

Cut in with present.

DI. That's another thing, if you've had your fling, if you've done what you want to, you're much less likely to resent your children; it's bound to lead to an easier parent-child relationship . . .

Continue flashback.

SANDY. Do bring Jim, I'd love to meet him – I know it's all boring babies and so forth here, but Dave and I are still capable of wrenching ourselves back to our real personae, honestly – i.e., as opposed to Mindless Mum and Weary Breadwinner (though I don't mind telling you I'd give my eye-teeth sometimes to swap my role for Dave's). If we wanted to get out in the evenings Dave would sit – he actually doesn't mind doing it. Well it's all right for him, I don't suppose I'd mind either if I'd escaped for the previous nine hours of the day!

And if we wanted to spend an evening all together, I promise . . .
I'm very good at bundling them off out of the way, when the need
arises.

*Fade to flashback. SANDY's house. Interior. Baby crying in SANDY's
arms.*

SANDY (*cries of greeting*).

DI (*Sounds of her arriving*). Sandy . . .

SANDY. Oh, Di, oh it's so lovely to see you! Oh hang on a minute,
I'll put him down.

DI (*strained laugh*).

*Baby's crying recedes but continues in background for part of
following.*

SANDY (*returning*). Well, now! Well, you *do* look good! That's a
very nice sweater!

DI (*relieved, relaxing*). Oh, thanks! I got it in Paris, I was there on
an assignment last month.

SANDY. You didn't bring Jim!

DI. Well, no, he's got to work after all, this weekend . . .

SANDY. Oh, I know that syndrome – Dave's just the same; you never
see them, it's all left to you. However hard they try to help, it's just
that, isn't it, helping out, in the end it's down to you?

DI (*bit shocked*). Oh, no, Jim's not like that! He does everything,
shops, washes; he's a really good cook – you should taste his chicken
tandoori. He's ever so sweet, he always does the food whenever we
have people to dinner. He says, 'You put your feet up darling and
have a gin, you've been wearing yourself out all week acquiring
us this lovely lifestyle' – see, he absolutely acknowledges my equal
contribution! And then he just saunters into the kitchen and flips
a few things together and comes up with these wonderful aromatic
concoctions – and everyone sits there slavering, and he stands there in
his pinny and they ask me where I got him from, this gorgeous little
treasure . . . He is fantastic, though . . . I mean, I call myself a feminist,
and I know I'm really lucky to have a man who can respect that.

Pause.

Baby winges a bit but is settling.

Did I mention, we're getting married?

SANDY. No . . .!

DI (*quickly*). For financial reasons, purely. Though we're very
committed. Thing is, I could only commit myself to someone

who completely understood my need for autonomy. And he does. He says the last thing he's having is me being dissatisfied. Well, he says, let's face it, it wouldn't do him any good, I'd only go off and leave him, and anyway what he wants is a fully-developed person for a partner, not a cabbage! I know I'm really lucky, having him understand so well.

Pause.

I mean, it's not marriage, in itself, is it? It's what you make of it. We've lived together long enough now to be quite clear about where we stand with each other. And well, we felt that while we're at it we might as well save money and beat the taxman . . . So's he's perfectly clear: I'm not having kids.

Baby starts crying again and continues in background.

(*Apologetic*). Jim is working, but actually, to be honest he isn't into the heavy domestic scene . . .

SANDY. Don't blame him. Who is? Neither am I.

Cut to present. Interior.

DI. You know, the paradox is that having had my fling, I can go on having it, I don't have to get into the heavy domestic scene. I mean look at all these labour-saving devices I've acquired down the years, and which you didn't have, the tumble-dryer, the electric mixer, the microwave . . . God, I remember, those times I came to stay, you were constantly rushing off to hang up the washing. I thought we'd never get out anywhere – and the nappies hanging in the bathroom: you couldn't have a bath without one giving you a cold wet slap in the face! (*Pause.*) They had disposable nappies then didn't they? I suppose you couldn't afford them . . .

SANDY. You're not kidding. They cost a bomb.

DI. Well, that's it. I'm damn lucky that that won't be a problem for me. Or proprietary baby foods . . . all that sieving you used to do by hand! I used to think you were pathetically besotted, all that time you used to hang around the pram and the high-chair, I used to wonder why I'd bothered to come, I couldn't get you to sit down and have a proper chat with me. I realise now it was just all the ruddy hard work you had to do! I don't suppose you could even buy additive-free baby foods in those days . . .

SANDY. No, you couldn't.

DI. Things have changed . . . (*Pause.*) Not to mention the fact that of course I'll have a nanny . . . (*Pause*). I know that's one unavoidable large expense . . . I mean, Jim's worried about the difference a nanny's salary will make to our bank balance and therefore our lifestyle, but as

I said to him, it's the nanny who will save our lifestyle if anything's
going to . . .

Pause.

Let me show you the buggy.

Sound of rummaging.

DI (*muffled*). It's here somewhere . . . it should be . . . ah yes!
Here it is.

Sounds of buggy being pulled out of cupboard.

There!

Silence.

What do you think?

SANDY. Yes . . . yes, it's fine . . .

DI. I mean, it's pretty well used, but it's quite an advanced model.

SANDY. A smear or two of yoghurt . . .

DI. Oh, no, that's just dust from the cupboard, I think.

SANDY. It's like mine –

DI. Oh, no it's not! No, this one doubles as a carry-cot. You had to
have a separate carry-cot, didn't you? It's got fold-up wheels – you
carry the cot without, you wheel it with –

SANDY. My carry-cot had those.

DI. Ah, but this whole thing folds up and goes away into the boot, the
cot-frame and all. And it's much lighter, look, it's special lightweight
tubular steel . . . And then later the whole thing converts into a
pushchair. You turn a screw or two. It's got flexible screws, it's
really quite ingenious – quick twist of the spanner and hey presto
it's a pushchair. And you're spared the expense of a second piece
of equipment . . .

SANDY. Oh well then you wouldn't have wanted mine.

DI. It's the ultimate all-purpose totally-convenient baby transporter,
specifically designed for the changes in women's lives.

SANDY. Well, I haven't seen one before . . .

DI. Things have changed quite a lot, haven't they? I mean, there have
been radical changes, in women's lives. It's a question, isn't it, of
taking advantage of these changes, and simply refusing to let a baby
take over your life? I mean, this buggy would be absolutely no bother
on public transport – well, luckily of course I've got my car; but
think of planes. This would slip quite easily into a hold. I've told
Jim: he really needn't get in such a state, I'm absolutely not letting
this baby stop us taking our usual holiday abroad next Easter. He

said: I'm not dragging a baby on holiday, I mean it is sweet of him to bother to think of the problems, but I honestly think I can prove to him that things just aren't as problematic nowadays.

SANDY. I must get back, actually. It's a good two hours' drive, and the kids will already be home from school . . .

DI. See, look at that! There are your children already, letting themselves in after school! Doesn't time fly? It doesn't last, does it? And here are you free to amble home when you please!

SANDY. Hmm. Well, not exactly. They don't like it actually. They feel insecure if I'm not there fairly soon after school. I guess they never got used to it, I never went back to work for long enough.

DI. Hmm. Well, I guess that's where I'm lucky. I won't be setting my family up with the wrong expectations, I'm going to be able to start the way I mean to go on . . .

Crossfade to hospital ward. Sounds of DI *in final moments of painful labour.*

Crossfade to present. Interior. DI's *home.*

DI. You know, Sandy, it's incredibly good of you to come. I mean, Jim would have had time off, he was perfectly prepared to – it's awfully sweet of him, he had this deal he was about to close, and of course it had to be in Paris, and as they say it's the big one, it's a contract his firm have been fighting for for years; and then last month their major rivals went to the wall, and they had to jump in while the going was good, and then Jim's been the key man in the negotiations all along – it would almost certainly fall through without him. Well, you might know, mightn't you, it would all come together the week after the baby was born! And he was prepared, under the extreme circumstances, to let it go! I mean, when I found I wasn't coping. Honestly, I'd never have guessed – this feeling so weak – you don't realise, do you?

SANDY. No, you don't.

DI. And when I almost fainted carrying her up the stairs – well, it would have been a dreadful sacrifice, but he was terribly sweet, he agreed to phone and cancel . . . But then of course, I thought of you. (*Pause.*) It really wasn't too much trouble, was it?

SANDY. Look, don't worry, just a clinic appointment of James's that was a slight problem – but . . .

DI. Honestly, I really didn't expect it, the physical incapacity. Thank God it doesn't last. I'm getting stronger every day – did you hear what the doctor said, he's never seen anyone heal up quite so quickly? But did you hear what he called me? Miracle Mum! That's the attitude, isn't it, that it's abnormal not to be an invalid. You can just see it, can't you? Parturition as the first step towards being treated as if you've lost both your arms and half of your brain! And irritating, really, the way they've been so cautious about my age. I mean yes, I'm pretty exhausted, but basically I'm as fit as a fiddle – God, I've had an easy life, that's just the point, I've had time and resources to look after my health; I'm fitter than a lot of mothers half my age. I'm not staying in the house any longer, no matter what the doctor says. Let's put the buggy together and go out.

Fade down.

Fade up rummaging in cupboard.

DI (*grunting etc. She's not up to it*). It's here somewhere . . . No . . .

SANDY. Di, let me do it . . .

DI. No, it's OK . . .

SANDY. Look Di, sit down. Let me.

DI (*emerging*). It's hard to accommodate this . . . being too weak to do things yourself . . .

SANDY (*muffled*). Can't see it . . .

DI. Right in the corner, it should be . . .

SANDY. No . . . Oh yes! Here it is!

Rattles, etc.

SANDY (*emerging*). There!

DI. Oh that's not all of it.

SANDY. Oh!

DI. It's come apart . . . there's another bit somewhere.

SANDY (*muffled again*). Can't see anything . . .

DI. Try the left-hand corner –

SANDY. Oh, is that it?

DI. Let's see . . . oh, yes!

Sound of rattling, buggy being dragged out.

SANDY. There!

DI. Oh great! Thanks, Sandy.

Baby begins to cry in background and worsens throughout the following.

DI (*distracted*). Oh . . .

SANDY (*turning to buggy*). Well, let's see . . .

Sound of buggy being assembled throughout.

Looks like this bit fits on here . . . and that bit goes there . . . Do you think that goes there?

DI. Let's see . . . Oh dear, I'll have to go and feed her –

SANDY. I can't make out if it goes here or here.

DI (*retreating, distracted*). There should be an instruction leaflet somewhere . . .

Sound of rummaging in drawer at far end of room.

Yes, here it is!

(*Returning.*) Can I leave it to you a mo, while I feed her?

SANDY. Sure!

DI (*still distracted*). Won't be long . . .

Fade up sound of buggy still being assembled.

DI (*returning*). How are you doing? Oh, I'm sorry to leave you to it. It's hard to get used to not being able to get on with anything . . . you don't realise . . .

SANDY. No, you don't. I've got this frame together but there seems to be something missing just here. I think it might be a screw . . .

DI. Well, they should all be there . . . No, that's right.

SANDY. It looks loose.

DI. I told you, this is it, that is the screw –

SANDY. It doesn't look the least bit like a screw.

DI. It's a new kind, I told you, special screws that swivel round so the frame can go in different positions, and fold completely flat.

SANDY. Ah! Ah well, in that case, this goes here, and that goes there . . .

Fade down.

Fade up, same.

SANDY. There! That's the whole thing complete!

DI. Great! Take the carry-cot off, and let's see how the frame folds.

Sounds of effort and squeaks.

SANDY. It doesn't seem to.

DI. Oh, there must be something wrong! You must have put it together wrong somehow. Let's see – no, it won't. Where did you go wrong? Let's see the instructions . . .

Fade down.

Fade up, same.

DI. No, that's right, you don't seem to have done anything wrong.

SANDY (*suddenly*). It's here!

DI. Where? What?

SANDY. Here!

DI. Where?

SANDY. Here, look on this screw! It doesn't give like the others, it's holding the whole thing jammed!

DI. Oh yes! Let's see . . .

SANDY. It's gone rusty, that's why.

DI. Oh dear!

SANDY. Oh don't worry, it's no problem, it's easily fixed, have you got a spot of oil?

Fade down.

Fade up, same.

SANDY. There!

Clatter of buggy closing.

DI. Ah! Good, isn't it? See the way the handle tucks away?

SANDY. Right, I'll just get this carry-cot cleaned up a bit now.

DI. Yes, it is rather dusty . . . Is that mould?

SANDY. Oh, it's nothing.

DI. That looks like cake . . . Is that a smear of yoghurt? And what's that? Oh, dear, it does look rather used.

SANDY. Right . . .

DI. Well, as I told you, she did really use it, well, you never saw her without it; ironic really, she got the latest model, designed for women's freedom, but like you, even then, only five years back, she couldn't get maternity leave. It took her years to get back on the career ladder. Once she left to have a baby she was tied to her eminently portable pram.

Fade down.

Fade up, exterior, street sound.

SANDY. Shall I push it for you?

DI. No! Goodness me, if I can't push this lightweight thing! I'll push it. (*Pause.*) Stupid, really, I have to admit to this sneaky feeling of pride . . . look at her . . . (*To baby.*) Hello there . . . are you still awake

then? Are you going out for a walk then? What can you see? Are
you looking at the lamp-posts? Can you see them? Can you? What
are you doing then . . . hey? (*To Sandy*.) Look at her looking.

SANDY. I remember being pushed in my pram.

DI. Do you?

Interior monologue.

SANDY. We were going down a leafy road. People noticed and they
stopped – you couldn't miss it, a pram like a carnival float. 'Oh what
a lovely baby,' they said, peering in the pram. And then they turned
to my mother: 'That baby has your exact same smile.' 'What a pretty
dress,' they said to my mother, 'you do look nice today.' My mother
smiled, gaining approval, the pretty neat mother well and truly fixed
in her pretty neat place.

Fade up street sounds, normal acoustic.

DI. It's gone cold.

SANDY. The sun's gone in.

DI. I'll put the extra cover over . . .

Cross fade, street scene continued.

DI. This is the shop . . . I've never used these little local shops
before . . .

SANDY. I'll hold the door.

Sound of struggle as DI tries to get pram up step.

Here, let me –

DI. It's more awkward than you'd have thought –

SANDY. Well, it's such a steep step –

DI. And it's such a narrow door –

SANDY. We could dismantle it –

DI. She's gone to sleep now, we'd only disturb her . . . Not as simple
in practice, is it?

SANDY. Well, it's such a small shop, it's such a short visit, it's hardly
worth it anyway. I'll wait outside.

Interior monologue. Background sound of rain in street.

DI. I stayed outside. It was raining. 'Stay there,' she said. 'Don't let
strangers put their heads in.' She went in. There were raindrops on
everything, clinging to the steely-cold pram-handle, running down
the metal plates near the door. 'Smith and Simon', it said. 'Solicitors'.
The rain dribbled in the S's, in the *Simon* and the *Smith* and the two
in *Solicitors*, snaking its way down. She was gone a long time. I was

wet and cold. Inside the pram, the baby was looking round, listening to the sound the rain was making on the pram-hood, I stuck my head in, the way you weren't to let strangers, and listened too.

Fade up appropriate sound briefly to surreal effect. Dip abruptly under sharp slapping sound.

She slapped my legs.

Background street. Rain sound dipped under:

Coming up behind me. 'Don't do that,' she snapped, 'you'll tip the pram up.' And then she wheeled it round, spun it round, balanced the whole great thing on one wheel, and it floated, flew, like a boat in all that flying water; for a moment it felt as if it might take off into the air, and drag us with it, hanging on. But then she steadied it, and off she went, and I ran, splashed after, leaving the offices of Smith and Simon, Solicitors, and I looked up and saw that it wasn't rain on my mother's face, but tears.

Fade up street sound. Present.

Add occasional pram squeak under following.

SANDY. Let me push.

DI (*though she's tired*). No, no . . . look, she's awake again . . . . What are you looking at? Are you looking at the bushes? Can you see some funny shapes then? Oh, look, she's moving her mouth. Are you sticking out that tongue of yours? What are you trying to do then? What are you trying to do with that mouth? It's as if she's trying to mimic me! I used to think women were mad talking to babies this young! You do, don't you?

SANDY. You do.

DI. Before you realise, before it happens to you . . .

SANDY. Yeah.

DI. You don't expect it, do you?

SANDY. No.

DI. The minute you set eyes on them.

SANDY. Yeah.

DI. Seems so soppy from the outside . . . No doubt it's just hormones, behavioural imprinting . . . but it's kind of devastating, isn't it?

SANDY. Yes it is.

DI. You think beforehand it won't happen to you . . .

SANDY. Yes you do. (*Pause.*) Look, let me push.

DI. Thanks. I would never have expected to get so tired, just walking this little way . . .

SANDY. Oh, well, it's normal, you do . . .

DI. But I can't get used to it . . . And this feeling . . . well, so stupidly vulnerable and emotional . . .

SANDY. You do.

DI. It's just not *me* . . . Thank God it's just a passing phase. (*Pause.*) Hasn't the wind gone cold? Do you think she's warm enough?

SANDY. Oh, I should think so.

Brief pause.

Street sounds. No squeak.

DI. Do you hear that? (*Pauses while they listen during following.*)

SANDY. What?

DI. The pram's squeaking.

SANDY. No, it's not.

DI. It is. It was.

Pram begins tiny squeaking.

DI. There! It *is*!

SANDY. All prams squeak, as far as I know.

Brief pause.

Street sounds with pram squeaking faintly. During following squeak grows (to represent DI's growing fear).

DI. That wheel looks wonky!

Pauses while they look during following.

SANDY. Where?

DI. There! That one!

They stop.

SANDY. It looks perfectly straight to me.

DI. It was wobbling. Move on, and then you'll see.

They move on.

DI. There, see!

SANDY. No. It looks all right to me.

DI. Surely, look, see how it's wobbling!

SANDY. They all are. It's the flexible screws, it's part of the design . . .

DI. No, that one's definitely wobbling more . . .

SANDY. I can't see it . . . I don't think it is, you know . . .

DI. You're probably right . . .

Pause as they walk.

Squeak growing.

DI. Though don't you think the cot's leaning over more to that side?

SANDY. No . . . I don't think so . . . no . . .

DI. I'm sure it is, you know . . .

SANDY. I'm sure it isn't.

DI. Perhaps you're right . . .

Squeak has reached surreal proportions. Cut.

Fade up interior.

DI. Out you come, then! That was your first walk out, wasn't it?

Interior monologue.

SANDY. We went home. Home for tea. Perfect mother, perfect baby, walking home in a hazy brown-bread-commercial summer. My mother parked the chariot under the tree. And went indoors, to the still dark suffocating shadows of a domestic interior . . .

DI. Out you come! Oh, feel her, she's cold! Feel her hands! Perhaps that mattress is rather thin. I should have lined it with more blankets . . . I never thought of that . . . Sandy, feel her hands! Oh Sandy do you think she's all right? Oh, aren't her lips rather blue?

SANDY. No, Di –

DI. Oh, look, is it normal? What about her breathing?

SANDY. Di, she's fine, she's awake –

DI (*breaking down*). Oh, Sandy –

SANDY (*arms round her*). Oh, Di, she's perfectly OK . . .

Fade down.

Fade up present, continued. DI's home.

DI. You know, on reflection, I'm not happy about that buggy.

SANDY. Oh?

DI. No, I do think it's leaning. I know it's not really perceptible. But have you seen the way she always slips to that side?

SANDY. No.

DI. No? Well, that wheel worries me. The way it wobbles. I know it doesn't do it all the time . . . I just feel . . . well, she did use it to death you know, as I told you. I mean three kids she had, and they all went through it, the last one until he was really quite big. They probably put quite a strain on the joints. (*Pause.*) What if it collapses when she's in it one day? (*Pause.*) And anyway, it's got no spring – the way it joggles on the bumps, it can't be good for her being rattled about that way. It's one design fault I hadn't thought of . . . after all, it was the earliest model of its kind, and they're bound not to get it completely right straight away . . . And have you noticed, about its height – it's just at the level of exhaust-fumes . . . and dogs' noses – what if one snaps at her one day?

SANDY. I'd have given you mine but –

DI (*interrupting*). Well, it's men isn't it, who design these baby transporters, since up till now it's men who've got to design everything . . . But it's possible, with men in general getting more involved in childcare, the designs have improved . . . Perhaps I ought to get a new one, after all. I know Jim and I agreed we wouldn't go to any unnecessary expense, and it hasn't exactly passed me by that the price of these things is ridiculously over-inflated, but there's no point scrimping is there, if a little investment would buy you complete convenience and peace of mind?

SANDY. I'd have given you mine. But it fell to pieces long ago.

Pause.

Jim's late.

DI. Oh, didn't I tell you, that was him on the phone before to say he's got to come back on a later plane. It was sweet of him, he said he'd rush if I really needed him, but I said no, he needn't bother. It was the same the day she was born, I'd only just gone into labour and he had this call to Southampton. I said then, for goodness' sake, no go, remember what we promised ourselves, that we wouldn't let this baby disrupt our lives! Well, as little as possible. I had to be there, of course.

SANDY/DI (*laugh uncomfortably*).

Fade down.

Fade up. Department store.

DI (*leading, closer to mike. Out of breath, but eager*). The prams are on the next floor.

SANDY (*following*). I thought you said you wanted to wait and choose one with Jim?

DI. He's so whacked, poor thing, I decided not to drag him. You should see the mound of paperwork he has to come back to every time he's been abroad! And then the first day back they send him off to Leeds!

Fade down.

Fade up. Pram department.

DI. This one's nice, isn't it, with the see-through hood?

SANDY. Mmm . . .

DI. I think that's a really good idea. But what do you think of the material? It looks as though it might crack, don't you think?

SANDY (*dubious*). Maybe so . . .

DI. Ah, but now what about this one – it's got a padded footrest, I've not seen that before, good isn't it, for keeping their feet cosy?

SANDY. But might it get dirty?

DI. I hadn't thought of that . . .

SANDY (*a bit reluctant to point out difficulties: she can see it's going to be a long haul*).

Well, would it wash?

DI. I don't know . . . do you think it would?

SANDY. Well, look at the label.

DI. Can't see anything . . . don't think so. Maybe you're right. What do you think?

SANDY. I don't know, it's up to you. (*Pause. Beginning to get irritated, trying to push things along.*) Well, if it doesn't wash . . .

DI. Hmm.

Pause.

I'm not sure. (*Pause.*) Hey, look at this!

Fade down.

Fade up. Department store café.

DI. What do you think?

SANDY. I don't know, Di.

DI. Well I think I like the coloured one best. All those different colours on the one buggy! You wonder why no-one has thought of it before, don't you? It's so obvious, babies need to be stimulated. I mean, that stultifying brown I've got her in now! Amazing isn't it, you get changes in ideas about child development, but it's quite some while before they get practical application . . . It's really nice, that, don't you think?

SANDY (*hardly caring*). Yes . . .

DI (*upset*). Don't you think?

SANDY (*trying hard*). Well, you know what you want Di, I can't make your mind up for you.

DI (*pathetically*). But it doesn't have a see-through hood . . . what do you think?

SANDY. I feel boggled, Di –

DI. I am very taken with that one with the telescoping frame . . .

Fade down.

Fade up. Pram department.

DI (*recovered*). It's very impressive. See, it slides and then clicks into various positions. You don't need a spanner, you can do it on the spot. A variety of shapes, and at any conceivable angle, it's ideal for any size of child, at any age. It says here the padding comes off for hot days. Oh look what it says: the extra-light padding is a by-product of space technology – about time, I say, that men applied advanced technology to domestic concerns.

Baby starts to make early hunger sounds and gets progressively distressed during next speeches.

What do you think? It's ideal isn't it?

SANDY. It seems very good . . .

DI. What do you think? Should I take it?

SANDY. Look, she's getting hungry, hadn't you better leave it, and come back tomorrow? Take the leaflet home with you, you said you wanted to discuss it with Jim –

DI. Oh, no, he trusts my judgement, he's always respected my judgement in everything. I think I'll take it. Yes, I will. It's the best one I've seen – the perfect combination of portability and security; real practical application of the concept that people can't just stick around at home to service babies . . . I'm sure when Jim sees it he'll approve . . .

Fade down.

Fade up. DI's kitchen.

DI (*entering*). That was Jim on the phone!

SANDY. Will he be long, dinner'll be ready in half an hour . . .

DI. You won't believe it – he can't make it, they've asked him at the last minute to take some clients out to dinner. Honestly, not content with sending him all over the face of the earth and then when he's here keeping him in the office ten hours a day, they feel they've a right to his evenings too – and they've the cheek to call that perks!

SANDY. Did you tell him you got the buggy?

DI. Oh well no, he was in such a rush – God, I wouldn't want to talk about buggies either, if I was that hassled . . . No, he'll see it in the morning . . . Do you think it's OK?

SANDY (*surprised*). Yes, it's fine . . .

DI. You don't think I should have got the one with the transparent hood . . .?

Fade down.

DI's *house. Morning.*

SANDY. What did Jim say about the buggy?

DI. Oh, well, he didn't really have time . . .

SANDY. Oh, I thought I heard you talking . . .

DI. Well, he did have a meeting starting at eight-thirty; I mean, for God's sake, *I'd* be irritated if someone accosted me on the way to an early important meeting and started on about the finer details of baby transporters – well, me, I'd be downright bad-tempered; I don't have anything like Jim's patience and forbearing . . . Oh no!

SANDY (*alarmed*). What?

DI. There's a chip in the paint on the buggy! Well, can you believe it? All those sophisticated features, and they slip up on an obvious fundamental! I'm taking it back. I'm not standing for that. What do they think people are? Do they think you'll be so blinded by technological development, you'll be fobbed off with a basic flaw like that? (*Pause.*) I like the one with the see-through hood, anyway . . .

SANDY. But that was even more expensive . . . I mean if Jim –

DI. It's nothing to do with Jim!

SANDY. What?

DI. The money . . . I mean the money.

SANDY. Oh . . .!

DI. Well, I did make the decision without him . . . Well, it's not an expense he ever agreed to, is it? Well, it's me that's got a thing about the old one . . . it's me that's got to push it . . .

Pause.

(*Very upset.*) It's all down to women, isn't it in the end?

SANDY. Yes, it is.

Interior monologue. Background sound of rain, maybe swelling as passage progresses.

DI. She's crying, really crying now, walking away from the offices of Smith and Simon, Solicitors, and what with the tears and what with the rain, she can't see; at the next kerb she stumbles, and the pram slips away, down the camber. Stupid girl, I try to pull it, but it's heavy, it slips off without me, it threatens to drag me; for one moment I see the baby's face looking at me, surprised, and then it disappears from view as I fall. I'm drenched. I've grazed my knee. 'Get up, girl,' she snaps. I'm crying. I'm causing trouble, I'm the cause of all the trouble . . . She rescues the pram which she'll push around on her own; she'll struggle round ever more on her own, a bulky pram, a whining girl, a troublesome vulnerable baby without all of which she might have kept him, that man, our Dad, whom we hardly ever saw again.

Cut rain sound abruptly. More normal acoustic, though closer, more significant than in previous naturalistic scenes (signifying greater honesty).

I always said I'd never repeat that pattern.

Pause.

No kids. It was a bargain between us. We promised each other. He promised me. I thought at the time I wanted that more than him. He thinks I've tricked him. I have.

SANDY. Oh, Di!

DI. Well, it was a mistake . . . but then . . . I had been thinking . . . I mean, I did forget to put my cap in . . . but you know . . . biological clock ticking away . . . (*Pause.*) He says it was my own decision. It was, it was me who kept insisting everything would be all right. He says it's my problem. He says it's not a problem he ever agreed to having. (*Pause.*) Have you noticed how he always avoids having her put in his arms?

Interior monologue.

Bird song in background.

SANDY. I was sitting in my pram, being pushed down a leafy lane. It was sunny, it was warm. It's a memory. It's not just hazy brown-bread-commercial fantasy. There is warmth in the memory, not just from the sun on my legs, but in my mother smiling, in my mother's love . . . We go home. My mother parks me beneath the big shady tree. And goes inside, to the cool dark peaceful house, and I'm secure, knowing where she is, and knowing I only have to kick and she'll come straight out again . . . I kick. The pram squeaks. Her head pops out. She comes to me, smiling.

MOTHER (*murmurs to baby*).

Sound of baby chuckling.

MOTHER. Hello, hello darling . . . hello.

SANDY. It is this you remember: that simple certainty of love, which you dare not remember, long to remember, and recapture, and make again. 'Oh what a pretty baby,' they say, 'see how she mimics you, that baby has got your exact smile.' My mother smiles into the pram. She holds out her arms.

MOTHER (*background murmurs, etc*). C'mon . . . c'mon . . .

SANDY. I hold out mine, mimicking, I look up into her face, smiling, mimicking; I am her and she is me. We are one.

Fade birdsong.

Present.

DI. You can understand it, can't you, how a man can feel shut out of it? And Jim – it's happened out of his control, almost behind his back, you can understand he feels alienated and angry . . . (*Pause.*) But I don't want to repeat the pattern. I don't want her to grow up thinking a father is someone who's never around . . . You can just see it can't you? Those male designers of baby buggies have every reason for streamlining women's child-caring lives.

Fade down.

Fade up. DI's house.

DI. It's been so good of you, Sandy, to come. I want you to know that I really have begun to appreciate the sacrifice. I mean I've come to understand how truly difficult it is for women not to end up shouldering the burden of children – don't think I don't see it, the irony of you picking up the pieces here, I do – it's our cultural conditioning we're fighting, isn't it, and the structure of our society, which hasn't changed all that much when it comes to the crunch. I mean, now I understand that children are the crunch. And I know what a sacrifice it's been for you to leave your children . . . I do hope they're OK . . .

SANDY. Oh, don't worry –

DI. But, actually Sandy, what if one of them were ill? And here you've been all these miles away . . . And didn't you say something about James having a clinic appointment. . . .?

SANDY. No, don't worry, Dave has taken time off – (*realises what she's said.*)

Pause.

DI. Oh . . . Oh, I see.

Fade down.

Fade up.

DI. Dear Sandy,

Happy belated Easter!

We had a lovely time in Morocco – I told Jim we'd manage it, and I proved it! I can't deny it was hard work – I had to boil water on a primus stove in the hotel bedroom for baby-food, and there weren't the baby-sitting facilities we'd been led to expect, but we still had a lovely time! You were right – things do get better, and in spite of all the difficulties, needless to say we'd never send her back, she's so lovely. And Jim's so good with her now, and she absolutely loves him, I guess she's going to be a real Daddy's girl! By the way, would you believe it, I had to take the other buggy back! (Remember, the one with the transparent hood?) We were crossing this square on holiday and the damn thing dropped to bits! Really – the whole thing collapsed. Metal fatigue – jagged metal sticking out everywhere. I'm thinking of suing the manufacturers, I mean, I dread to think what injury it could have done to a baby! Luckily, as it happened, though, she'd been being dreadful – wouldn't stay in the pushchair a moment (the heat, I guess) and I was pushing it with one arm and carrying her with the other. You should have seen me, standing there with everyone staring, arms full of a baby and a mass of collapsed metal. I couldn't make Jim hear, he'd gone on ahead, you know what he's like, he's got such a wonderful sense of adventure . . .

O ANANIAS, AZARIAS AND MISAEL

by Jennifer Johnston

For Caroline, Rosaleen and Stella
with thanks

Jennifer Johnston was born in Dublin in 1930, the daughter of Denis Johnston the writer and the actress and director Shelah Richards. Since 1970 she has had eight novels published, one of which, *The Old Jest*, won the Whitbread Prize and another, *Shadows on Our Skin*, was shortlisted for the Booker Prize. She has almost finished her ninth novel. She has written two full-length plays, *Indian Summer* and *Triptych*, and five short plays: *The Nightingale and Not the Hawk* (The Peacock Theatre, Dublin and Druid Theatre, Galway); *The Porch* (Gaiety Theatre, Dublin); *The Invisible Man* (The Peacock Theatre, Dublin); *O Ananias, Azarias and Misael* (BBC Radio 4 and The Peacock Theatre) and *Billy* (BBC Radio 4).

O Ananias, Azarias and Misael was first broadcast on BBC Radio 4, 'Thirty Minute Theatre' on 20 April 1989.

NARRATOR   Stella McCusker

Director: Jeremy Howe
Running time, as broadcast: approximately 30 minutes

Aye that's it then.

All red up.
Some people would just walk out of a place, slam the door behind them.

Aye there's ones like that would never give a second thought to the dust to the grime.

I couldn't do a thing like that, I couldn't let strangers come in here and find things to point the finger at.

Strangers. God knows there's been enough of them around in the last couple of weeks.

Gawkers every day.

I've watched them driving down the wee lane, slowing down their cars when they get to the gate. A couple stopped, stopped dead there by the gate and stuck their heads out of the windows.

I was affronted.

Curiosity killed the cat.

I wanted to open my door and shout down the path at them . . .

Curiosity killed the cat.

My mother always used to say that to us when we were kids.

I didn't believe her.

I never saw too many dead cats around the place.

I remember my brother once shot one with an air gun.

Killed it . . .

That wasn't very nice.

He didn't realise . . . you know about death and that. He didn't mean to hurt it you see. Just thought . . . I don't know what he thought, but I know he didn't mean to harm it.

He never touched the air gun after that.

I haven't seen a lot of him over the years.

His wife's a decent woman, but they don't have much time to spare. She works, and what with that and the wains she's tired. You know . . . washed out.

Fair do's to them they came down to the funeral.

Aye. Fair do's.

I don't know how he . . . oh yes . . . cats – it's funny the way your mind works. It flies around . . . or maybe it's just mine.

It's probably just mine. I've never been what you'd call clever.

I don't understand a lot of things.

I like the telly though.

I like to see people's faces; here in the room. Sometimes it is full of people's faces.

You'd never be really alone if you had the telly. That's what I always used to think.

It's not like that though.

They don't notice you, those people there.

They don't care about you.

Why should they after all?

They have their own lives to lead . . . their own problems.

I mean to say some of them run the world.

It's odd to see the people who run the world right here in your room.

They make it all sound so important . . . and then I feel foolish because I don't understand it . . . I mean about the Middle East and that . . . I don't understand . . . I don't suppose it matters whether I do or not.

It's a funny thing, people's shoes don't creak nowadays.

When I was a child, people's shoes used to squeak.

It means they haven't paid for them, my mother used to say.

She was from the South, my mother.

She had funny notions.

You couldn't believe everything she said.

I'm sure that Mrs Thatcher's shoes creak.

I don't know why. I always get that feeling when I look at her on the telly, I think to myself, I bet your shoes creak.

I said it to Billy once. . . .

To Billy.

He howled.

He laughed a lot.

He liked to laugh.

Billy.

Easy amused.

I used to say that to him.

Billy Maltseed, you're easy amused.

My name is Christine.

Billy and Christine.

We had that written in silver letters on our wedding invitations.

It looked very smart . . . and bells . . . you know sort of ringing sideways . . . and a couple of wee angels . . . lovely.

Yes.

That was a lovely day.

I have the pictures . . . everybody smiling.

Only my granny wouldn't come up from Carlow. She said she might be shot.

God, but we laughed at that.

I was a bit sad though.

I loved my granny.

You'd think she'd have taken the chance.

A bit too old for adventures, Billy said.

You never know when you're happy.

I often wonder if Mrs Thatcher's happy . . . or the Queen. I don't like those glasses she has to wear . . . they make her look cross.

I love to see her in the crown and all that, but the glasses spoil it.

I wonder if she knows.

I wonder if she watches herself on telly. Perhaps she doesn't have the time.

I wrote to my cousin Doreen, she was one of my bridesmaids . . . Well I wrote to her the other week and told her I might come down to live near her. She's married and has two wee boys, well they were wee when I last saw them, they must be . . . getting into their teens now . . . Her husband is in the bank in Kilkenny. A nice enough fellow. I went down once to visit them, several years ago. It was Billy insisted I go . . . to take my mind off things, he said. It was the summer I went to the hospital to have the tests. Doreen had the two wee fellows then, little pets they were.

It made me sad to see them. Isn't that a silly thing to say?

I never had the heart to tell Billy what they said at the hospital . . . I just let him think it was my fault . . .

You know the way some men are . . . they get very hurt about that sort of thing, ashamed. I'm not sure why. Men feel more ashamed than women. I think so.

That's why I never told him the truth.

It was hard sometimes not to let it come bursting out . . . you know when we had a wee row or something.

Old Mrs Maltseed always went on about it.

Well Christine, no news for us yet?

I just used to smile at her, but sometimes I felt I could do her an injury.

She was a rough sort of a woman . . . right enough she'd had a hard life, out here in these hills, managing, trying to make ends meet, keep a look on things.

Never a speck of dust there was in this house. You could have eaten your dinner off the floor.

No amenities in those days either.

We put the bathroom in . . . Imagine that! No bathroom and a toilet out in the yard when we came here . . .

I couldn't live like that, I said to Billy.

You may be used to it, but I'm not . . and I had the old man to look after and all . . . all that washing extra.

Sheets. Every day there were sheets and his pyjamas . . . that was later on of course. Not to begin with. I didn't know then the way things were going to go with him.

To give him his due, he worked hard when he was able.

I must say Billy was very good . . . he got that job with the Area Board driving the school bus and fitted it in with the farm . . . He was never lazy, never one for sitting round and letting things get the better of him.

We never did anyone any harm.

That's what I said in my letter to Doreen.

I couldn't understand why she didn't want me to come.

A short holiday perhaps, she said, after all the fuss has died down . . . but then you'll have to stand on your own feet.

I didn't ask to stand on hers did I? Haha . . . Haha.

It was like as if she thought I had some dreadful disease that I was going to spread around, contaminate her family, those two nice boys . . . Fred . . . Kilkenny city . . . the Allied Irish Bank . . . the whole country maybe.

Contaminate.

I wouldn't want to go there if she felt like that.

I wrote and told her that.

We never did anyone any harm.

We kept ourselves to ourselves. I'm not saying I didn't have any friends . . . I did. I had friends all right.

We didn't say much to each other, but we were friends.

It's quite lonely here in the winter.

The nights seem very long.

Billy was good company, I have to say that and there was the telly.

I had a good friend who was . . .

Dolores O'Kane.

Lives just down the road.

The bungalow down the hill with the red roof.

He was cool enough, but I liked her.

We had the same problem . . . the father in law.

You can laugh.

That's what we used to do . . . have a laugh. You have to have a laugh from time to time. Not at anyone's expense of course, just at things . . . you know, things in general.

That's what we used to do, have a cup of tea and a laugh.

She has kids . . . that's a help . . . It makes you look into the future . . . see some . . . hope?

Perhaps I shouldn't say hope.

I think I'd feel some hope if I had children.

Maybe not.

We always used to talk about the children we would have.

Well in the early days we did.

I suppose it's as well under the circumstances that we didn't have any children.

Think how they'd be now.

Orphans.

No . . . they wouldn't be orphans . . . they'd have me.

I'd stay here if I had children.

I'd work my fingers to the bone.

My mother always said a bit of hard work never hurt anyone.

I'd have loved a wee girl.

Some nights I used to hold him, close in my arms and rock him. If I shut my eyes I could imagine it was a . . .

He never knew that was what I was thinking.

So many things we didn't say to each other.

I suppose everyone's the same.

Filled with secrets.

The doctor said just to tell him to go along to the clinic.

It's probably very easy to deal with Mrs Maltseed, he said.

He was very nice.

I just didn't have the heart to tell Billy.

I suppose I was wrong.

He liked to play the big guy. You know . . . tough guy Billy Maltseed.

That was what he liked about the Lodge . . . all those men . . . preening themselves. I used to laugh to myself when I saw them, beating their drums, marching, flags, all that sort of thing.

I used to wonder what they were like inside, under the clothes and the sashes.

I said to him once, turn a bowler hat upside down and guess what you could use it for?

He wasn't all that amused.

We are not amused my mother used to say when I did something silly.

We are not amused.

I put the sashes in the coffins with them. . . . His and the old man's. I didn't want to see them again. I thought the Minister might say something, but he didn't. Maybe he didn't know.

My mother was Church of Ireland.

I don't think I'm anything at all.

I used to love the Church of Ireland when I was young.

O, let the earth bless the Lord, yea, let it praise Him and magnify Him forever.

That one I liked.

Oh Ananias, Azarias and Miseal, bless ye the Lord . . .

They don't sing things like that in the Presbyterian Church.

Praise Him and magnify Him forever.

I asked Billy once why they didn't and he said . . . we did away with that sort of rubbish a long time ago. We speak direct to the Lord. That's what he said.

I didn't believe him.

I was lonely for Ananias, Azarias and Miseal.

Whoever they were.

I never knew who they were, but I could see them, walking with me, their great wings folded behind them.

Great feathery wings.

I miss their company.

Matthew, Mark, Luke and John bless the bed that I lie on.
Every night before I go to sleep I say that.
And if I die before I wake . . .
I didn't tell Billy.
. . . I pray the Lord my soul to take.
I don't see any harm in saying that.
Even when I held him in my arms and pretended he was my little
baby . . . even then I used to sing that in my head . . . Matthew, Mark
. . . and if I die before I wake, I pray the Lord my soul to take . . .
He never knew.
He thought I thought like him, believed like him.
Listen . . . you can hear Dolores' children playing in the field.
I used to give them apples from our apple tree . . . They had none
of their own.
The children used to come and steal fruit at night.
They enjoyed that much more than me giving them fruit.
That's children for you!
I was going to train as a teacher and then I met Billy.
Where's the point he said?
My mother had taken the cancer then and was weak in herself.
She just said suit yourself child, but don't forget the five wits God
gave you.
I never knew what they were.
She'd have liked me to be a teacher all right. I knew that.
I could see that in her face.
Billy was such fun.
I can't wait forever he said.
There's plenty of good fish in the sea, my mother said, but I
liked Billy.
We never had a row, in all those years. Well hardly a row, not like
other people have.
Twenty.
Next May.
Yes.
Twenty.
He said he'd take me away for a holiday.
To celebrate, you know.
Twenty years is a good long time.
He got those books from the travel agent.
I threw them in the bin the other day.
Where's the point now?
I wouldn't want to go on my own.
Dolores went to Spain last year.
She said it was great . . . as long as you didn't touch the food.
She said people were coming down in hundreds from the food.
I didn't fancy Spain myself.
I thought Switzerland would be nice, but he said it was a bit expensive
. . . or Vienna. That's the place where they have those lovely horses.
I've seen them on the telly.

They dance.

I'd like to have gone and seen those horses . . . but that was about the time when the old man got bad and we couldn't go anywhere.

I thought we should have put him in the hospital . . . he'd have been well looked after there.

Dolores' father-in-law is in the hospital . . .

They go to visit him once a week. She brings him biscuits.

He likes ginger biscuits. He dips them in his tea.

My mother never let me do that.

Your teeth will rot in your head if you eat slops like that she used to say.

Billy wouldn't hear of it.

My father's going into no home.

We can mind him.

We!

I laughed a bit when he said that . . . inside myself of course.

He hasn't long for it, we can manage. He said that to the minister. There was a nice small place run by the church for old people like him. But Billy had his mind made up. I went up to the hospital one day with Dolores when she went to visit. There were six of them all in the one room. I think he'd have liked that. A bit of company. The nurses seemed decent enough. Jokey you know.

He's still going strong.

Maybe old Mr Maltseed would still be going strong if . . .

If if's and and's were pots and pans there'd be no need for tinkers.

She used to say that too.

If . . .

It was the shock that killed him.

If only . . .

I had to tell him . . .

There wasn't anyone else really.

I thought of asking the minister, but I didn't think it would be right.

Unkind to have such words said by a stranger.

There's been Maltseeds in this house for over two hundred years.

I suppose some people thought it was time for a change.

That's a joke, in case you don't recognise it.

I don't really mean that.

I said it to Dolores the day after the two funerals.

She didn't think it was funny.

Then of course I realised I shouldn't say that sort of thing to her.

She's been a good neighbour.

A good friend, no matter what people may say.

There are times you should keep your mouth shut.

Hold your tongue.

When my mother used to say that to me, I'd to put my tongue out of my mouth and pinch it between my thumb and finger . . . like this. I'm sure you remember doing the same thing.

She'd laugh.

Rapscallion, she'd say.

I never heard anyone else use that word.

It's a great word, isn't it?

Rapscallion.

It's a very cheerful word.

If I'd a had kids, I'd have called them . . .

Dolores says that everything is sent by God.

I can't see it like that.

Why would he send me such sorrow?

What have I ever done to him?

I am such a small person. I can't believe he can even see me when he looks down from the sky. I'm not like those people you see on the telly.

I asked Dolores that . . . she didn't know the answer either . . . unless . . . of course . . . it's because I'm a Protestant . . . but that can't be right, because so many of the others suffer too.

I didn't ask the Minister because I don't think he likes me very much.

I get that feeling from him.

I went to him the time Billy first said he was going to join the Regiment.

I asked him to have a word with Billy . . . to say something to him . . . but he wouldn't. He said he thought it was a very good thing that Billy should join . . .

I said to him . . . but Reverend the Bible says we mustn't kill people.

Dear Mrs Maltseed, he spoke in a sort of dry little voice, I hope that it will never come to that. I'm sure, he said that Billy will not allow himself to be carried beyond the bounds of duty by bigotry or over zealousness.

I remember that . . . over zealousness.

Isn't it funny the way some people talk.

I suppose he got a word like that from the Bible.

The Good Book, he used to call it.

They try to hide things sometimes in the way they talk.

I think our Minister's a bit fond of the sound of his own voice.

Dry little voice, like it hurt him to speak.

I suppose I could always go back to the Church of Ireland now.

I hadn't thought of that before.

Oh Ananias, Azarias and . . .

I'll have to get a job.

. . . Misael.

The money for the house won't last forever.

Maybe they'll come back and walk beside me.

I never had a job.

It's a nice wee house, after all we've done to it . . . and fifty acres.

No one wants to live round here.

Dolores' husband offered to take the land . . . but who'd buy the house without the land.

It's been well looked after all these years.

People are afraid now.

People like us are afraid.

That was why he joined the Regiment.

A lot of his pals joined it years ago, but it wasn't till Sam Hickson was shot he decided to join himself.

Where's the point I asked him?

I mean he wasn't cut out to be a soldier.

And why bring trouble on yourself.

Why be a hero?

He was wild upset when Sam was killed.

Sam was a good friend of his.

They'd been to school together.

They were in the same Lodge.

He had a bit of a problem with the drink and he spent a few nights here when he was too full to go home to his wife. When he wouldn't have been able to find his way home to his wife, put it like that. But he was decent enough.

Lived down near the lake.

I didn't tell anyone about Billy joining the Regiment . . . like my cousin Doreen, I never told her.

They have odd notions in the South . . . but then she saw it in the papers and she was all upset. That's one of the reasons they don't want me down there . . . at least I think it is.

I didn't tell Dolores either . . . but she just said to me one day . . . came right out with it . . .

Is your Billy in the Regiment?

Just like that. I was over having a cup of tea in her kitchen.

Oh aye . . . he is.

I couldn't tell her a lie.

Part time, I said.

She never said a word.

She just gave me a funny look.

There's no harm in it I said.

I didn't think there was any harm in it.

I don't think Billy thought there was any harm in it either.

A duty. Aye.

A duty.

I think they had a bit of crack too.

Like wee boys.

I didn't think your Billy'd do a thing like that.

She said that to me about a week later.

Like what?

I asked, but I knew.

You know well she said.

It's only road blocks and the like, I said.

She gave me another funny look and passed me a piece of cake.

She's very good at making cakes.
She brought me down one of her fruit cakes the day before the funeral.
Rich dark fruit cake she makes . . . like my mother used to.
Old fashioned.
You don't get them like that in the shops.
My mother never bought a cake in her life.
Nothing would have persuaded her.
The day I can't make a cake myself is the day we stop eating cakes.
Of course in her last few months she didn't want to eat anything at all.
Turned right off food.
Faded away.
Big eyes staring out of her head and she couldn't keep her teeth in her mouth.
I was affronted every time I saw her.
O ye children of men, bless ye the Lord.
She was a good woman.
I loved that woman.
My heart was broken watching her die.
I suppose you could say that Billy was saved that.
He didn't know what hit him.
That's what the doctors said anyway.
I wonder.
It was a wonder that none of the kids in the bus were injured.
I suppose whoever done it wouldn't have cared.
I shouldn't say that.
I shouldn't feel like that, but sometimes I can't help it.
I have asked God to fill me full of charity, but he hasn't had time yet.
I had to identify the body.
That seemed so silly to me, didn't everyone know that it was Billy Maltseed drove the school bus.
I didn't want to see him.
I said that to them, but they paid no heed.
It's the law missus.
It seems a silly law to me . . . to persecute someone like that.
I didn't want to see him at all. I just wanted him to be nailed up in the coffin so that I could remember him, held tight in my arms like a baby.
I can't see that any more.
The other picture gets in the way.
I wondered and wondered whether to tell the old man, but I was afraid that with all the fuss going on and the people in and out and the press banging on the door he might get troubled. He used to get troubled and cry when he didn't understand what was going on.
So I went up to his room and I told him.

I don't think he understood to begin with, he just lay there smiling and googling . . . that's what I used to call it . . . googling.

He used to wave his head from side to side and make this funny noise.

But he must have known what I said because half an hour after, he took this terrible turn. By the time the doctor came he was gone.

When Dolores came round with the cake I told her about it.

Two for the price of one, I said.

I shouldn't have.

Sometimes a little joke lifts your spirits.

She looked most upset.

You shouldn't say things like that, she said.

Why don't you have a good cry. Let it all come out, she said.

I couldn't.

I just couldn't cry . . . not because I didn't want to, just the tears wouldn't come out of my eyes.

Billy's sisters cried. They came to the funeral and bawled all over the place.

I never shed a tear.

I felt terrible.

You're being very brave Mrs Maltseed.

Rotten, dry little voice and he spoke his prayers in that rotten voice and I still had dry eyes and all those officers and Orange men and the MP were there and they all spoke to me and my eyes were bursting out of my head with pain and I still couldn't cry.

You probably saw the funeral on the telly.

I sat and watched it that evening on the news after everyone had gone home . . . How strange I thought to see myself there on the telly.

I really do exist, that's me there, walking, standing, shaking hands . . . that's me. I am a real person.

. . . And then I cried, when I saw myself there with all those people.

Dolores didn't come to the funeral, being an RC.

I could hardly have expected her to.

But she's been very good ever since.

I mean she pops in every day to see if I'm all right. Brings me little bits of this and that . . . some cold ham, a bit of pie.

She's a good woman.

I'll miss her.

I'll miss this place.

My brother's found me a wee place in Belfast.

Just big enough to swing a cat in, he says.

I'm a bit afraid of Belfast, but, as my mother would have said, you can get used to anything if you try.

I thought I might try for a job in Marks and Spencer, somewhere nice like that.

What with the compensation and the bit of money from the house, I'll be all right for a while.

I don't like leaving Billy.

I hope he won't mind.

After all, why should he? He'll have Ananias, Azarias and Misael for company now.

Dolores says she'll pop in to see me whenever she comes up to Belfast.

That'll be nice.

She can tell me how things are going on here.

I think it's some friend of Dolores' husband is buying the place.

I heard that round.

That'll be nice for the children. They'll have other kids to play with.

It's a bit lonely out here.

Oh Ananias, Ázaris and Miseal, bless ye the Lord.

Praise him and magnify him for ever.

It's time I went.

The bus passes the end of the lane in ten minutes.

I wouldn't want to miss it.

I hope I haven't taken up too much of your time.

Goodbye.

The Stalin Sonata was first broadcast on BBC Radio 3, 'Drama Now' on 1 August 1989. The cast was as follows:

MARIA LVOVNA DZERZINSKAYA	Barbara Jefford
SEMYON PAVLOVITCH	Clive Merrison
MIKHAIL KARLOVITCH	Philip Voss
PAVEL ILYITCH	Ian Targett
SOPHIA IVANOVNA (Doctor)	Jane Leonard
STATE PROSECUTOR	Donald Gee
JAILER	Brian Miller
PIANIST	Mary Nash

Director: Richard Wortley
Running time, as broadcast: approximately 70 minutes

Note: All of Maria Lvovna's speeches are internal, *that is, spoken in her thoughts, and not aloud.*

THE STALIN SONATA

by David Zane Mairowitz

For Geraldine

David Zane Mairowitz was born in New York City in 1943. After studying drama at the University of California, he moved to London in 1966, where he edited for a time the *International Times*. His published books include *Bamn*, *The Radical Soap Opera*, *In the Slipstream* and *Wilhelm Reich for Beginners*. Several of his stage plays have been produced in London, including *Flash Gordon and the Angels* (Open Space) and *Landscape of Exile* (Half Moon), and his radio plays are broadcast regularly by the BBC and in ten other European countries. He has lived in the South of France since 1982, currently in Avignon, and has two children, Liesl and Avril.

Time: 1938
Place: Moscow
Music: W. A. Mozart, Sonata for Piano in A minor K. 310

Scene 1

A 78 rpm recording of the 'Internationale' in Russian. When it finishes, various dials are switched off.

PAVEL ILYITCH. How was I?

MIKHAIL KARLOVITCH (*whispering*). Master switch.

PAVEL. What's that?

MIKHAIL. The master switch. You're still on the air.

Switch off.

MIKHAIL. You must never forget that, Pavel Ilyitch. The radio audience will hear every word you say. They wait for it.

PAVEL. I thought they switched off as soon as the 'Internationale' comes on.

MIKHAIL. There are those who listen to the silence that comes afterwards, hoping the announcer will accidentally leave his microphone on, so they can catch him saying: 'Enough for those bastards tonight,' or 'I've been dying for a pee for two hours.' They sit there with open notebooks, even for half an hour in front of a silent radio, hoping for some political remark or an indiscretion from our private lives.

PAVEL. What for?

MIKHAIL. What for? (*Hesitant.*) Sooner or later these things . . . turn up.

PAVEL. Where?

MIKHAIL. In . . . letters to the editor . . . on someone's desk . . . somewhere . . . in some ministry or other . . .

PAVEL. Is that why the previous announcer was dismissed?

MIKHAIL. Your predecessor? No, that was different. He stumbled.

PAVEL. Stumbled?

MIKHAIL. Bumbled. Slipped up. While saying the words: 'This is Radio Moscow wishing you a good night in the struggle against social fascism and counter-revolutionary elements.'

PAVEL. What did he say?

MIKHAIL. He said 'elephants'.

PAVEL. What for?

MIKHAIL. Slip. Of the tongue.

PAVEL. It could happen to anyone.

MIKHAIL. No. It mustn't. It nearly cost *me* my job.

PAVEL. How did I say it?

MIKHAIL. A bit too close to the microphone. You made it sound too intimate.

PAVEL. It was my first day, Mikhail Karlovitch. Tomorrow will be better.

MIKHAIL. Another thing. When you announce the names of the musicians before you play a recording . . .

PAVEL. Yes?

MIKHAIL. You must not give them equal weight with your intonation.

PAVEL. Why not?

MIKHAIL. Some artists are more important than others and must be given special vocal emphasis. For several, you are not permitted to mention their names.

PAVEL. How am I to know?

MIKHAIL. You have a list there on your desk.

PAVEL (*rustling papers*). I don't seem to find it.

MIKHAIL. Then my secretary has not finished altering it. It must be changed once a week, according to instructions from the musicians' union. You must never assume that someone's status will be as it was last week. It may well have been changed from 'exclamatory' to 'monotone', or will now be found under 'revered people's artist' or . . .

PAVEL. Or?

MIKHAIL. Struck off the list altogether.

PAVEL. Does this apply to the composers as well?

MIKHAIL. Only those who have the misfortune to still be alive. You may use your discretion with the dead ones.

Telephone rings.

MIKHAIL. You answer it. Tell her I'm delayed in traffic, that the building's magnetic door won't open. Anything.

PAVEL. Who is it?

MIKHAIL. My . . . mother?

PAVEL. Your mother?

MIKHAIL. I had to take her in because of the housing shortage.

PAVEL. Are you sure it's her?

MIKHAIL. I know her ring. There is no one else in Moscow who could make a telephone sound with such conviction.

PAVEL (*answering*). Central Studio. Radio Moscow.

MIKHAIL. I'm not here.

PAVEL. He's not here. Who? One moment please. It's Secretary Stalin.

MIKHAIL. It's who?

PAVEL. Secretary Stalin.

MIKHAIL. Stalin's secretary?

PAVEL. No, I don't think so. He said 'Secretary Stalin'.

MIKHAIL. Not 'Comrade Stalin' or 'Leader Stalin'?

PAVEL. No.

MIKHAIL. And . . . he wants to speak . . . to me?

PAVEL. The Chief of the Radio. That's you, Mikhail Karlovitch.

MIKHAIL (*takes telephone*). Lyubimov . . . (*Voice cracks gradually during conversation.*) I . . . yes . . . oh . . . yes . . . Secretary St . . . took so long?

Pavel Ilyitch packs his things, knocks over a glass.

Shut up, you idiot! What's that? To you? Oh no no, Secretary St . . . It was the cleaning woman . . . No way to speak to a worker? Certainly not, Comrade Secretary. Out of the question. It was a subordinate shouting at her. His name? Surely you don't need to take up your time with such trivia, Comrade Secretary. I'll reprimand him myself . . . His . . . name.

PAVEL. Not me, please.

MIKHAIL. His name is . . . Ivanov. Alexandre. What? Send you a recording? Of course. In the morning. By limousine. With pleasure.

Mozart, yes . . . I know it, yes, yes . . . (*hums a bit of melody*.) Excellent choice, Your Excellency. What? Did I say, 'Your Excellency'? I meant to say, I meant to say: 'An excellent choice, your excellent choice was, Comrade Excretary.' What? No, I couldn't have said that. I only hoped to say that your command is my wish, excellent Secretary . . . You'll have the Mozart first thing . . . Yes? In that version? Are you sure? I mean, of course you are sure, but, you know, we have so many excellent renditions of that same sonata . . . Dzerzinskaya Maria Lvovna. Have it? Of course we have it, Comrade Secretary, we have all recordings in our archive. It's just that . . . wouldn't you prefer. . . .? No, no, the Dzerzinskaya version is – how can I put it – an excellent choice. We are all extremely thankful for your choices. Thank you, Your Secretary, it was your pleasure. By nine o'clock. Yes, an excellent good night to you.

Hangs up telephone.

PAVEL. What have you got there, Mikhail Karlovitch?

MIKHAIL. My cyanide tablet. I managed to save it all through the storming of the Winter Palace some twenty years ago, then during the British invasion, the whole of the Civil War in the grimiest hours when the Whites gouged out the eyes of anyone even suspected of being a Bolshevik. I always kept it ready to swallow, hidden in this little amulet round my neck, but I never even needed to remove the covering. Until now.

PAVEL. Because I made too much noise?

MIKHAIL. What's that? No, no, no. (*Desperate*.) He wants Mozart. By morning. In the famous Dzerzinskaya version.

PAVEL. Maria Lvovna Dzerzinskaya?

MIKHAIL. Exactly.

PAVEL. It's a good choice.

MIKHAIL. Too good.

PAVEL. How does she stand on the list. 'Exclamatory' or 'monotone'?

MIKHAIL. She isn't on the list. What are you doing?

PAVEL. Looking for her recording.

MIKHAIL. Don't waste your time, Pavel Ilyitch.

PAVEL. I'm looking under 'D'. There are no references to Dzerzinskaya in the index. Nor any recordings.

MIKHAIL. Of course not. I destroyed them all two years ago.

Scene 2

MIKHAIL. I know it's after midnight, Semyon Pavlovitch, but you are the only one who can help me.

SEMYON PAVLOVITCH (*after a time*). How do you know it wasn't a prank?

MIKHAIL. A prank?

SEMYON. Someone calling and claiming to be . . . him.

MIKHAIL. Who would do such a thing?

SEMYON. It might be an enemy.

MIKHAIL. I have no enemies.

SEMYON. We all have enemies, Mikhail Karlovitch.

MIKHAIL. You mean, someone might have been impersonating him just to cause me grief?

SEMYON. Who knows? It's possible.

MIKHAIL. Yet . . . it is also possible that it was him. I don't know his telephone voice.

SEMYON. Yes.

MIKHAIL. And the question is: yes, it may, as you suggest, Semyon Pavlovitch, be . . . someone's attempt to injure me, or even just a practical joke, but the question is, the real question is: can I risk it?

SEMYON. I wouldn't.

MIKHAIL. The thing is, Semyon Pavlovitch, you wouldn't happen to have. . . .?

SEMYON. I got rid of them.

MIKHAIL. We all did.

SEMYON. And the original discs?

MIKHAIL. I incinerated them.

SEMYON. It was the thing to do. Then.

MIKHAIL. It would have been dangerous for the Studio to keep them.

SEMYON. Why does he insist on that version?

MIKHAIL. God knows.

SEMYON. God knows?

MIKHAIL. No, I mean, it has nothing whatever to do . . .

SEMYON. Can he have forgotten the Dzerzinskaya Trial?

MIKHAIL. He can't be expected to keep up with every arrest.

SEMYON. On whose orders did you destroy the discs, Mikhail Karlovitch?

MIKHAIL. Orders? There were no orders. As such. Not directly.

SEMYON. Pity. If you could prove you had been ordered to do it.

MIKHAIL. No one commanded it. It was just somehow . . .

SEMYON. In the air.

MIKHAIL. Expected. Or, not even expected, but . . .

SEMYON. It was your revolutionary initiative.

MIKHAIL. It was my duty.

SEMYON. Too bad it won't help you now. Why didn't you just say the recording was lost?

MIKHAIL. I didn't dare. He wanted to have it.

SEMYON. You could have told him the truth.

MIKHAIL. The truth?

SEMYON. Yes.

MIKHAIL. That I smashed Dzerzinskaya's records?

SEMYON. Two years ago it was the correct thing to do.

MIKHAIL. But now he wants to listen to one of them.

SEMYON. And for breakfast, you say?

MIKHAIL. He is at his *dacha* just outside Moscow. He was suddenly taken by a fit of . . . melancholy, he said . . .

SEMYON. That's bad . . .

MIKHAIL. . . . and he remembered suddenly the Mozart sonata in the Dzerzinskaya version which always used to comfort him.

SEMYON. I haven't got it, Mikhail Karlovitch. I honestly can't remember if I cracked mine in half or tossed it away in a snowdrift. Like you, I didn't want it one day to be found at my place.

MIKHAIL. I thought that you, Semyon Pavlovitch, as Chief of the Musicians' Union, you have the ear of the Minister of Culture . . . He might listen to you and plead my case with . . .

SEMYON. Even if that might help – and I doubt it – I can't wake up the Minister this time of night. I'd have to do it first thing in the morning. And then it might be too late.

MIKHAIL. What shall I do? I'll lose my position as Chief of the Radio. I have to support my mother. You have to help me, Semyon Pavlovitch.

SEMYON. No I don't. It goes against my grain to help anyone.

MIKHAIL. For old time's sake.

SEMYON. Especially not.

MIKHAIL. Then I'd better hand in my resignation.

SEMYON. Have you thought of sending him another version?

MIKHAIL. Of the sonata?

SEMYON. Then you'd only have to print a new label and paste it on. He doesn't know the first thing about music. He'll never know the difference.

MIKHAIL. The problem is. . .

SEMYON. Yes. I know. He just might.

Scene 3
Heavy keys opening lock.

SEMYON. You have been alerted by the Minister of Culture, Jailer?

JAILER. He woke me up.

SEMYON. Then I may go in?

JAILER. Go in? There? What do you expect to find?

SEMYON. I was informed that the prisoner Dzerzinskaya was in your charge here.

JAILER. We have many prisoners here. Too many. This one was lucky. She had a hole to herself. That was a privilege.

SEMYON. I want to see her.

JAILER. You may see only straw.

SEMYON. Is she dead?

JAILER. I don't know.

SEMYON. How can you not know?

JAILER. I haven't seen her for some time.

SEMYON. How can that be?

JAILER. With a certain class of prisoner no spoken contact is permitted. Even for me. I slip a tray of food inside the door. Sometimes it's eaten, sometimes not. For several weeks, I've taken it away untouched.

SEMYON. Why don't you go in to see?

JAILER. I've other things to attend to.

SEMYON. Such as ?

JAILER. The prison volleyball court needs whitewashing.

Pause.

SEMYON. Can I go in?

JAILER. Have you got a handkerchief to cover your mouth and nose?

SEMYON. Let me in. We're losing time.

Cell door opens.

JAILER. Hurry up. I've my tea in five minutes.

SEMYON (*inside*). Is there light in here?

JAILER. Do you know the cost to the State of a light bulb, Comrade Union Chief? Or the electricity that goes into it? In times like these.

SEMYON. A torch? Matches? Wait a minute. I've some in my pocket.

Match struck. Some seconds pass.

Jailer?

JAILER. Comrade Union Chief?

SEMYON. There is an old woman lying here. Dzerzinskaya would be twenty years younger.

JAILER (*laughing*). Is she dead?

SEMYON (*match struck*). Ice cold. But her breath has blown out my match.

JAILER. Bad luck.

SEMYON. Are you sure this is Dzerzinskaya?

JAILER. It was her two years ago when she went in.

SEMYON. Why have you left a woman to rot in here?

JAILER. Women are treated as equals here. Except, in her case, if she'd have been a man, she'd have been shot long since.

SEMYON (*match*). Maria Lvovna. Masya. (*Pause*). Jailer, call an ambulance at once.

JAILER. In the middle of the night?

SEMYON. When else?

JAILER. They'll never come.

SEMYON. Say it's on the orders of the Minister of Culture.

JAILER. They won't have heard of him. You'll have to leave it until morning, and then wait your turn. You'll be lucky to get one before the day after tomorrow.

SEMYON. Then help me carry her out to my car.

JAILER. Her?

SEMYON. Yes, her.

JAILER. She is a prisoner here.

SEMYON. The Minister of Culture . . .

JAILER. Is not the State Secretary for Prisons.

SEMYON. He has authorised that the prisoner be released for one night.

JAILER. For one night?

SEMYON. You'll have her back in the morning. You have my word on it. The Minister of Culture has agreed to take responsibility.

JAILER. I have to have written confirmation.

SEMYON. You'll have it.

JAILER. Two months in advance. And with the official seal of the Ministry. And signed by the State Secretary for Prisons. And notarised.

SEMYON. I need her now.

JAILER. Surely you can do better, even at this time of night, Comrade Union Chief.

SEMYON. Look, Jailer, I want this prisoner. You have my word that she'll be back before nine o'clock.

JAILER. Leave me your Party card.

SEMYON. What?

JAILER. As security. Your Party membership card. And two hundred rubles.

SEMYON. Are you . . .

JAILER. My expenses. And if she isn't back here in time, I'm going to bandage my head and say you took her by force.

SEMYON. Yes, yes.

JAILER. These people are not supposed to come out of here once they go in. It's for ever, Comrade Union Chief.

SEMYON. Don't worry. I'm only borrowing her.

Scene 4
Recording studio set up. Piano tuned in background. Microphones placed, etc.

SEMYON. You understand, Sophia Ivanovna, I must be able to count on your absolute discretion.

DOCTOR. I'm a doctor. That goes without saying, Semyon Pavlovitch.

SEMYON. I didn't mean to question your professional qualities, Doctor. It's just that we're dealing with an exceptional case.

DOCTOR. The Minister of Culture explained it was to help an indisposed musician before embarking on a concert tour.

SEMYON. Something like that.

Sound studio noises. Pavel Ilyitch setting up.

MIKHAIL (*entering*). We are ready, Semyon Pavlovitch.

SEMYON. We are not.

MIKHAIL. It's half past one.

SEMYON. We're doing our best, Mikhail Karlovitch.

DOCTOR. Which is your musician?

SEMYON. On the couch. In the Studio there.

DOCTOR. That woman?

SEMYON. That woman.

DOCTOR. I see.

SEMYON. I trust you have some cortisone in your bag.

DOCTOR. Cortisone is rationed. It's only for extreme emergencies.

SEMYON. This is one.

DOCTOR. That will be for me to decide.

SEMYON. Doctor, I need that woman to play a Mozart sonata. And to record it. Before dawn. Do you understand?

DOCTOR. No.

SEMYON. Then you'll have to accept my word for it. Your job is to get her on her feet.

DOCTOR. I have to examine her first.

SEMYON. Is this really necessary?

DOCTOR. Yes.

SEMYON. Can't you just give her an injection of something that will set her in motion?

DOCTOR. This is a human being, not a steam train.

SEMYON. Yes, that's perfectly sweet to say, but tonight I need a pianist who will run like a steam train.

DOCTOR. You'd better find another doctor, Semyon Pavlovitch. There are plenty of them sitting behind desks in the Ministry of Health who would gladly oblige you.

SEMYON. I'm not trying to tell you your trade, Sophia Ivanovna, only to impress you with the urgency of the case.

DOCTOR. All cases are urgent.

MIKHAIL (*entering*). Semyon Pav . . .

SEMYON. We're just coming.

MIKHAIL. The piano has been tuned.

SEMYON. But not the pianist.

Fades into studio. Irregular breathing of Maria Lvovna.

SEMYON. Well, Doctor?

Studio noises.

DOCTOR. Isn't there somewhere else I can examine her?

SEMYON. We don't have the time.

DOCTOR. It's extremely irregular.

SEMYON. Her breathing?

DOCTOR. That too. You say you want this woman to play a sonata?

SEMYON. Yes.

DOCTOR. Tonight?

SEMYON. That's right.

DOCTOR. Out of the question.

SEMYON. Don't say that.

DOCTOR. I'm sorry. I can cure people, but I don't work miracles.

SEMYON. We are not even asking you to cure this person, Doctor. Simply to make her . . .

MIKHAIL. Piano-ready.

SEMYON. Yes.

DOCTOR. Give her five months in a rest home and then maybe – just maybe.

MIKHAIL. You don't seem to understand, Doctor.

DOCTOR. Nor you, Mikhail Karlovitch. For one thing, her fingers have been broken.

Silence. MIKHAIL KARLOVITCH *whimpers. Sounds from* MARIA LVOVNA.

SEMYON. Are you sure?

DOCTOR. You can see the fissures around the knuckles.

SEMYON. Are they broken now?

DOCTOR. They seem more or less healed. But look how she winces when I bend them. Is that painful?

MIKHAIL. She doesn't answer you.

DOCTOR. No. So far, not a word.

SEMYON. I've heard of experimental pain killers being administered to steel workers with arthritis, and their production quotas remain impressive.

DOCTOR. She is also suffering from exhaustion and exposure. Is there no heating in this place?

MIKHAIL. It's not permitted after eight o'clock.

DOCTOR. She must have at least some blankets round her legs.

MIKHAIL. I'll send for them.

DOCTOR. And a meal.

MIKHAIL. A meal?

SEMYON. Doctor, you must understand . . .

DOCTOR. Semyon Pavlovitch, this woman has not eaten for days, perhaps weeks. She is suffering from malnutrition. Where do you expect her to find the energy to play.

SEMYON. In your syringes.

DOCTOR. No. At best, I might keep her awake. But she must be fed.

MIKHAIL. Where will we find food at two o'clock in the morning?

SEMYON. There is the White Russian restaurant along the boulevard.

MIKHAIL. It will be closed.

SEMYON. It's not closed. All Party officials go there secretly after midnight to drink. You must order a meal in the name of the Minister of Culture.

MIKHAIL. At once.

SEMYON. In the meantime, we can begin.

DOCTOR. I will not allow the patient to play before she has eaten.

SEMYON. A little warm-up won't hurt her, Doctor. It's been two . . . She's a little bit out of practice.

DOCTOR. She should have a hot bath before anything else.

SEMYON. This time I have to overrule you. We can have it prepared, and drop her in it when she's finished her job here. Not before . . . Come now, Maria Lvovna, I'm going to help you to the piano. That's it. I'm sure you'll be delighted to see this baby grand after . . . your little absence. That's it. Let's sit you down on the stool, make you comfortable. I know it may seem strange to you . . . to be called out of retirement at such short notice, but it's not often that an artist is given a chance to launch a new career . . . overnight, as it were.

DOCTOR. She doesn't answer you.

SEMYON. To be frank, Doctor, her hands interest me more than her voice tonight.

DOCTOR. Careful, she's keeling over.

SEMYON. I've got you. That was close. (*Shouts*). You, in the control room. Bring us a chair. This stool won't do.

PAVEL (*through microphone*). There's a wheelchair in the first aid closet.

DOCTOR. That would be better.

SEMYON. Bring it.

PAVEL. Right away.

SEMYON. I'll just hold you here, Maria Lvovna, until the comfortable chair comes . . . She has no weight.

DOCTOR. Strange. Because she's not unusually thin.

SEMYON. Just weightless.

Chair brought in.

So. There you are. Now you can concentrate on the keys. Just let your hands run over a few scales for old time's sake. Here, I'll help you place them. Now.

Piano thumped.

Surely you can do better than that.

Piano thumped.

DOCTOR. Why doesn't she speak, I wonder?

SEMYON. She's shy in the extreme, Doctor. Always was. She puts all her effort into her music and, when she's on form, hardly needs to spoil it with language.

DOCTOR. It might be because her mouth and lips are extremely dried out.

MARIA LVOVNA (*internal speech*). Because they feed you over-salted food and scarcely any liquid, and after a time your tongue sticks to the roof of your mouth and wants to live there. And now they expect me to speak when they have come to put me to sleep like a dog because they don't want it to get out that I died in prison, I still have my admirers in the world who will sooner or later ask about me, and they'll say: she died peacefully, leaning over her piano, exactly as she would have wanted it.

Scene 5
Maria Lvovna eating voraciously. Throughout the scene, and often in the play, she grunts or utters the sound of someone long starved of human company, who cannot judge the effect her vocal utterances have.

MIKHAIL (*whimpering*). Half-past two.

SEMYON. That's fine, Maria Lvovna.

MARIA LVOVNA *protests.*

DOCTOR. Why do you take her food away.

SEMYON. She's had enough, Doctor.

DOCTOR. A few mouthfuls is not enough.

SEMYON. That will do for the first movement.

DOCTOR. First movement?

SEMYON. The sonata has three movements. When she finishes the first, she can have more to eat. I don't want her to be so content that she will not oblige us with her talent. This way, Maria Lvovna, you'll have some Blinis to look forward to between the Allegro and the Andante Cantabile.

DOCTOR. This will keep her in a state of permanent anxiety.

SEMYON. That's what makes an artist function, Doctor. That's hard for you scientists to fathom . . . So, here's the sheet music, Maria Lvovna. Of course, you know this sonata by heart, but you may be a bit rusty. So.

Silence.

SEMYON (*quietly*). We want you to play, Maria Lvovna. I know you are tired, but you always said the touch of the keys could revive you, could save you from distress.

Sombre chord.

MIKHAIL. Impossible!

SEMYON. We're trying to help you, Maria Lvovna. This is surely what you've dreamed of these two years, the chance to play again, to be heard again.

MARIA LVOVNA (*internal*). Rehabilitation? It does happen. They say it happens. From time to time. But what has it to do with him? Why him? Does he want to repent for what he did to me?

PAVEL. She's nodding asleep.

SEMYON. Doctor, I have to call on your black bag of wonders.

DOCTOR. This is not feasible. She must at least sleep the night through, and we will see what morning brings.

MIKHAIL. My head on a plate.

SEMYON. Calm youself, Mikhail Karlovitch. Doctor, you were recommended to me by the Minister of Culture himself. He says you have a great career ahead of you, active in the Party youth organisation, that you have even applied to further your studies abroad.

DOCTOR. In Heidelberg, yes.

SEMYON. This is a very delicate matter these days.

DOCTOR. Somewhat.

SEMYON. Without the help of Brunov, the Vice-Minister of Health, my wife's second cousin, this would be unthinkable, no?

Scene 6
Piano chord. Awful.

DOCTOR. It's the fingers. She's clearly in pain.

SEMYON. Can't you do something?

DOCTOR. I've just given her something to wake her up, Semyon Pavlovitch.

SEMYON. A local sedative, perhaps. For the hands.

DOCTOR. Not in her condition. (*Pause*). Yes, all right.

MIKHAIL. She doesn't even react when you put the needle in.

MARIA LVOVNA (*internal cry, gradually blends into internal monologue*). . . . and when they finally came to step on my fingers with their boots, one holding my arms spread out wide, the other cracking them one by one, there was no pain then because they were already frozen from months in the cell, and went pop like icicles snapped off a shingle, and the two of them wondering out loud why the order was only for my fingers, worrying – they were only boys – that there might be some mistake and that they might get into trouble . . . so I reassured them that no, it had to be fingers for a pianist as it would have been lips and teeth for a bassoon player. . . .

During the last part of the speech, the first bars of the sonata are played, poorly, the music continuing after the monologue has finished.

SEMYON (*from control room*). Stop! Cut!

MIKHAIL (*whimpering*). Impossible!

The music continues.

SEMYON. Someone stop her.

PAVEL (*over microphone*). You can stop now, Madame.

Music continues.

SEMYON. Cut off the sound in here. This is killing me.

Sound from studio off.

MIKHAIL. What are we going to do?

SEMYON. It's the fingers. She can't seem to keep them upright. They keep rolling over the keys.

MIKHAIL. What shall I do with my life? I have no skills. I never learned to do anything. I'll have to drain the public urinals.

SEMYON. Doctor . . .

DOCTOR. This is a mechanical problem, Semyon Pavlovitch, not a medical one. Another injection won't help. The hands have lost their mobility. She needs to be reeducated in their use.

SEMYON. It couldn't be some muscular disorder quickly remedied?

DOCTOR. No.

PAVEL. Excuse me. I don't want to interfere . . .

MIKHAIL. What is it, Pavel Ilyitch?

PAVEL. It might just be possible to tie small wooden splints under her knuckles to keep the fingers at right angles to the piano.

MIKHAIL. This is absurd.

PAVEL. Just a thought.

SEMYON. Could it work, Sophia Ivanovna?

DOCTOR. I'm not a physiotherapist.

Scene 7

MIKHAIL. Why can't they hurry? We haven't recorded a single note yet.

PAVEL. It takes time to place each splint.

MIKHAIL. And she still has ten fingers.

PAVEL. Look how she watches them with her frightened eyes like a squirrel. She doesn't seem to understand what's going on.

MIKHAIL. It has to remain that way.

PAVEL. Why?

MIKHAIL. Why? Because . . . if she knew why we were doing this, she might not . . . cooperate.

PAVEL. You mean, she hasn't been told what it's for?

MIKHAIL. Certainly not.

PAVEL. I don't understand.

MIKHAIL. No one asks you to understand, Pavel Ilyitch. Just to cut a disc.

PAVEL. You can't expect too much of me, Mikhail Karlovitch. I'm an announcer, not a recording engineer.

MIKHAIL. There is no time to find anyone else. And, you know, Pavel Ilyitch, there are some wonderful positions here at the Radio and . . . one day all young aspirants long to read the news bulletins, that's where real pride comes in, anyone with limited intelligence can say: 'And now here's a Beethoven symphony, played by such and such an orchestra, directed by who cares,' but to announce the news, Pavel Ilyitch . . .

PAVEL. Perhaps even before it happens.

MIKHAIL. Who knows, yes, perhaps . . . the thing is . . .

PAVEL. What is the thing, Mikhail Karlovitch?

MIKHAIL. You are to keep your mouth shut about this. If anyone asks, we found one last copy of the recording stuck away in the archives for posterity, never intending to be played again on the air.

PAVEL. What if it's a trick?

MIKHAIL. A trick?

PAVEL. To see if you kept the recording instead of destroying it as you felt it your duty to do.

MIKHAIL. You really think so?

PAVEL. Perhaps you did the right thing two years ago, but now they're just checking up. And as soon as you hand over the recording, someone will ask: 'Why wasn't this destroyed?'

Scene 8
First movement of sonata, played slightly better.

MIKHAIL. The splints are working.

SEMYON. Just.

DOCTOR. I can't tell the difference, but I never studied music.

SEMYON. You don't need to study to hear that something is being abominably played.

DOCTOR. Perhaps she can't play any better than that.

SEMYON. She was the best.

Silence.

DOCTOR. What happened to her?

SEMYON. Her? Oh, you know. Men. Alcohol. Let herself go.

DOCTOR. Has she been on the streets?

SEMYON. Nearly. Very nearly.

Music suddenly stops.

MIKHAIL. Oh no! Just when we were getting somewhere! And in the middle of a refrain! (*Through microphone to sound studio.*) Why did you stop there, and not at the end of a line, so we could edit, Maria Lvovna?

MARIA LVOVNA (*internal*). It's just that the lice are springing from my hair on to the keys every time I play a crescendo, and they scamper down between the notes and I'm afraid of crushing them if I go on playing, after all, who else stuck by me all this time, refusing to disown me when everyone else did?

Scene 9
Towards end of first movement.

MIKHAIL (*in control room*). Almost there, almost there. Don't slow down.

PAVEL. She'll make it.

MIKHAIL. It's awful. Just awful. How can I possibly send him this?

SEMYON. He wanted Mozart in the Dzerzinskaya version. That's what he's getting.

DOCTOR. Dzerzinskaya? There was a counter-revolutionary criminal by that name who was also a concert pianist.

SEMYON. Coincidence.

Silence.

In any case, Mikhail Karlovitch, you've done your best. Perhaps the bad quality won't even be noticed.

PAVEL. We could scratch the record several times and excuse it that way.

MIKHAIL. Perhaps he won't even listen to it. Perhaps it was a whim that he'll forget by morning.

Music comes to an end.

PAVEL. She's done it!

MIKHAIL. It's only the first movement. And it's after four o'clock. Wind her up again.

DOCTOR. No, I forbid it. The agreement was that she eats and rests between movements.

MIKHAIL. Semyon Pavlovitch . . .

DOCTOR. Otherwise I leave the case. I won't be responsible for her collapse.

SEMYON. I did agree to this, Mikhail Karlovitch.

MIKHAIL. But there is no time.

DOCTOR. Look through the glass. She's fallen asleep on the keyboard.

SEMYON. Half an hour, Sophia Ivanovna, no more.

MIKHAIL. Half an hour? That leaves no time for re-takes.

SEMYON. Be glad you have anything.

MIKHAIL. Be glad? You tell me to be glad?

SEMYON. That's right. Imagine it was a command.

MIKHAIL. A command?

SEMYON. Yes. A command to be glad. Then you'd be glad.

PAVEL. More than pleased to be glad.

Scene 10
Voracious eating, animal sounds from Maria Lvovna.

DOCTOR. I'm sorry I had to wake you, but I thought you might want to eat before playing again . . . Not so fast. Don't gulp it down. You'll make yourself sick.

Eating noises.

This food is much too rich for you. Blinis and sour cream. When did you last eat, I wonder? Where have you been?

MARIA LVOVNA (*internal*). To London to look at the Queen.

DOCTOR. Why don't you answer? At first I thought there might be some throat damage, but I examined you and know this is not the case. And you make these sounds while eating. If it's a question of being surrounded by men, I understand. But they're in the control room drinking vodka. We're alone now. I'm a doctor. It would help if you would confide in me.

MARIA LVOVNA (*internal; external eating sounds as background*). They never sent a woman before, to see if I was fit to be interrogated further, why did they bother anyway, they were only sent in to say yes, except that one who wanted to study tropical medicine . . . he never touched me, only looked at my fingers and said he would recommend that I be released. My first thought was he had been made to say so to build up false hopes – the sadists sit at their desks and dream up such things. How often did they play my records through a loudspeaker in my cell before running the needle sharply over the grooves or cracking them in half. But I saw in that boy doctor's face that he was sincere, and I allowed myself for some brief seconds to hope, until I realised what it would mean for him, and then I begged him not to do it, not to recommend my freedom, he was so young, and anyway it was hopeless, but he continued to insist, it was his duty as a doctor to see that I was sent to a State hospital to recover, and I cried, knowing my own son would never have done the same, no, was content to denounce his mother, but how can I blame him, it was expected of him to turn against me . . .

MARIA LVOVNA *is sick.*

DOCTOR. I was afraid of that.

MIKHAIL KARLOVITCH *whining in control room.*

SEMYON (*through microphone*). Clean her up please, Doctor, we must continue.

MIKHAIL. Pavel Ilyitch, go and pour some disinfectant on the keyboard.

DOCTOR. She was eating too quickly. Boiled buckwheat would have been better.

SEMYON (*entering studio*). I'll remember that next time.

DOCTOR. Are you feeling better now?

MARIA LVOVNA *crying, exhausted.*

SEMYON. Come, let's move your wheelchair to the piano, Maria Lvovna.

MARIA LVOVNA *makes a sound of rejection.*

Be a smart girl.

Rejection.

Maria Lvovna . . . Masya. I'm trying to help you. We want to make this recording so that . . . the highest authorities might hear your talent again and . . . who knows? reconsider your case. We want to show what we've all lost in your absence. Don't turn against yourself in this delicate hour.

DOCTOR. I think she's too weak to continue. Her pulse is far below normal.

SEMYON. Give her another injection. We're losing time.

DOCTOR. I don't think . . .

SEMYON. Another injection, I said.

Scene 11
Piano plays second movement, heard throughout scene in control room. Liquid poured, glasses.

MIKHAIL (*suddenly hopeful*). It's nearly . . . acceptable.

SEMYON. By the last movement it might even be mediocre.

PAVEL. It must have been like this in the old days. I mean sitting in here, listening to her out there.

MIKHAIL. Except that then you couldn't take your eyes off her.

PAVEL. I expected her to be much younger.

SEMYON. She is.

MIKHAIL. She commanded absolute respect when she marched into the Studio, the engineers treated her like a goddess, never daring to speak to her. If one key were marginally out of tune, just ever-so vaguely, she'd say nothing, simply stand up and go home. And she never played a false note. In all the years, I can only remember doing one single re-take. It was in the middle of a Bach two-part Invention, I think. She suddenly fainted. The rumour had it that she was in love, even pregnant. You probably know more about that than I do, Semyon Pavlovitch.

SEMYON. I don't know anything.

Clink of glasses. Pause.

PAVEL. What did she do?

MIKHAIL. Do?

PAVEL. Yes.

MIKHAIL. She was accused of . . . convicted for . . . the details evade me now . . . Semyon Pavlovitch would know more . . .

PAVEL. I didn't ask what she was accused of. I wanted to know what she had actually done.

SEMYON. The question itself is absurd.

PAVEL. Why?

SEMYON. Because it presumes that life is either black or white.

PAVEL. I presume only that someone is guilty when they commit a crime.

SEMYON. You're too inexperienced to know better, Pavel Ilyitch.

Doctor enters room.

SEMYON. Ah, Sophia Ivanovna, can I offer you a drink?

DOCTOR. I never drink. And when I'm on duty, double never.

SEMYON. I have a special place in my heart for sobriety. It comes upon me in my more maudlin moments. I imagine my wife, my teenage sons, looking at myself as it were, with their eyes, with the same penetrating contempt, thinking: this is the only way he knows how to get through his grim day, he has no other means, as we do, sport, knitting, shopping, we the spiteful sober who know how to cover our tracks.

DOCTOR. In any case, you won't live long.

SEMYON. It's the hope in that thought which keeps me alive, Doctor.

The music suddenly stops.

MIKHAIL. Oh, my god, what now?

DOCTOR. Something is worrying her.

MIKHAIL. Why is she looking around like that?

PAVEL. She's afraid of something.

SEMYON. She has to pee. Can't you see that? Look at her squirming there. Doctor, go and help her, will you?

PAVEL. It's too late.

SEMYON. What's that?

PAVEL. Too late.

Scene 12
Pavel Ilyitch repositioning microphone.

PAVEL. This is really not my job, you see. It was badly positioned, the microphone. I'm only the announcer. I play the records. This is not my job.

Pause. Exaggerated breathing, throat clearing of MARIA LVOVNA.

I don't mind you not answering me, Maria Lvovna. (*Still working.*) I only wonder . . . the way they talk about you, there in the Control Room . . . Don't be frightened, I've disconnected the cable. They can't hear us . . . I only wonder . . . I can understand why you won't speak to them. But I ask myself how you can go on playing for them.

MARIA LVOVNA (*internal*). It's part of the punishment. It doesn't end with the judgement. It goes on. From time to time it stops for no reason. They suddenly remember you are still there and, perhaps because they have had no success in their work, or because a woman has snubbed them, or because a taxi sped by, splashing mud on their shoes, they come to take it out on you. On me.

PAVEL. I used to try to get a seat for your concerts, but they were always sold out. Of course, they weren't completely sold out, but I wasn't yet a Party member so there was no chance of getting a late ticket. Then, by the time I joined the Party, there were no more Dzerzinskaya concerts. Every spring I waited for the new programme, but you were no longer on it. And then, one night about three years ago, I celebrated the end of my studies with some friends in a bar in one of the cheap run-down districts in the suburbs of Moscow . . .

MARIA LVOVNA (*internal*). Stop!

PAVEL. There was a battered out of tune piano playing . . . you know . . . chansons . . . French rubbish, which we were supposed to think of as modern and . . .

MARIA LVOVNA (*internal monologue, with 'Sous Les Toits de Paris' played on piano, half-speed under speech*). It could have been worse, it was worse, once my concerts and recordings were prohibited, accompanying silent films of heroic Russian battles from the Middle Ages in urine-stinking cinemas. I had to feed my son, I would have played in a bordello if they had paid me, anything to keep playing, not to get out of practice, what was the alternative, to scrub floors with detergent and ruin my playing hands forever. What difference did it make, they are dead anyway. My hands. (*Internal, distressed.*) You, boy . . . you . . . please . . . some . . . cold cream for my hands and just caress my cheek with the back of your hand, not so they'll see it, so many years since anything but a fist touched my face, you, boy . . . he doesn't hear me . . .

PAVEL. I'm sorry you won't talk to me. Still, after what they've done to you. I understand.

MIKHAIL (*over microphone from Control Room*). Pavel Ilyitch, what's taking so long? Why don't you answer? Is the cable disconnected in there?

PAVEL. If you need anything, Maria Lvovna, whatever it is, just give me a signal. Discreetly. I'll do my best to help.

MARIA LVOVNA (*internal*). Help.

Scene 13
Piano playing second movement.

MARIA LVOVNA (*internal*). When it came, the first time, a fist in your face, you convinced yourself you were dreaming it. You spent a lifetime sheltered from pain, cultured parents who never slapped you, so that you'd fall from a swing, scrape your kneecap and imagine nothing could be worse. Or riding in official limousines from the country estate to the concert hall, passing brutal streets but thinking only of the fingernail that must not splinter because it would put you off your stride, or the special cream brought back from Switzerland, guaranteed to protect your hands from fungus. And then, when they came for you, you told yourself that it could not happen to you, not you, because . . . because . . . invent me a reason, Maria Lvovna. Because you were a woman, because you were Dzerzinskaya . . . because the wife of the head of the security police always took a subscription to your concerts, because . . .

Cuts abruptly into trial sequence.

Scene 14
External. Ceiling fan. All trial sequences heard 'internally' by Maria Lvovna.

PROSECUTOR. I declare this session of the military council of the State Tribunal now open. We will proceed with a reading of the indictment in the case of the State vs. Leskov, Grodowsky, Dzerzinskaya and others.

Fades into a window opening. Birds heard in the distance.

DOCTOR. Please close that window, Mikhail Karlovitch. This patient risks pneumonia.

MIKHAIL. Just for a moment, Doctor. To let in some air. It's so close here in the studio. And, frankly . . .

DOCTOR. Frankly?

MIKHAIL. That woman stinks. She hasn't been bathed for two years.

DOCTOR. Two years?

MIKHAIL. Perhaps they hose them down now and again.

DOCTOR. I order you to close that window.

Fades into trial sequence.

PROSECUTOR. The Accused Leskov: how do you plead?

LESKOV. I plead guilty to all the crimes I am accused of.

PROSECUTOR. The accused Grodowsky: how do you plead?

GRODOWSKY. Guilty.

PROSECUTOR. Of all crimes listed in the indictment?

GRODOWSKY. Guilty. Yes.

PROSECUTOR. The Accused Dzerzinskaya: how do you plead?

MARIA LVOVNA. I plead not guilty to the accusations against me.

PROSECUTOR. Not guilty?

MARIA LVOVNA. I'm a musician, not a spy.

PROSECUTOR. You deny having committed criminal acts against the Soviet people?

MARIA LVOVNA. I am not a criminal.

PROSECUTOR. The Accused Shebalin: how do . . .

SHEBALIN. Guilty.

PROSECUTOR. Of all crimes listed in the indictment?

SHEBALIN. And more.

Fades into studio. Ceiling fan.

SEMYON. Do you really expect her to play with that tube in her arm?

DOCTOR. This woman is too weak to continue, Semyon Pavlovitch. She can't take any food into her stomach without sicking it up again. I am attaching this glucose drip to her wrist so we can nourish her as we go along.

SEMYON. The hand must be able to move along the keys.

DOCTOR. I'll leave some slack. Where can I hook up this drip bottle so that it hangs above the piano?

PAVEL. There is nothing but the fan on the ceiling.

DOCTOR. You'll have to stop it turning.

MIKHAIL. We'll all perish from suffocation.

DOCTOR. It's for your sonata.

PAVEL. I'll get a ladder.

Fades into trial.

PROSECUTOR: Accused Dzerzinskaya: is it your intention to continue lying to the court and to contradict the testimony you gave at your preliminary hearing some months ago?

MARIA LVOVNA. Yesterday, I gave way to feelings of false modesty, and then, because of the difficulty of understanding the indictment against me, and due to my weakened physical state, I neglected to speak the truth. Instead of saying, 'yes, I plead guilty,' as I should have, I answered – mechanically – 'not guilty'.

PROSECUTOR. Mechanically?

MARIA LVOVNA (*'Sous les Toits de Paris' plays softly under speech*). I did not have the strength, in the face of public opinion, to speak the truth. I ask the court to consider my explanation, and to accept that I plead guilty to all the charges against me, and that I am completely responsible for my breach of the court's trust in me and for my treachery.

Fades into studio.

DOCTOR. This is going to hurt, but I must put this pin in your wrist so we can feed you through this drip. There. So.

Drip adjusted by switch.

This way you'll be able to finish your task here and go right home to sleep.

MARIA LVOVNA (*internal*). Home.

DOCTOR. Tomorrow, I'm going to recommend that you be transferred to my clinic.

MARIA LVOVNA (*internal*). What do they want? To experiment on me?

DOCTOR. Above all, you need to be nourished properly. But I'm concerned about reanimating your hands.

MARIA LVOVNA (*internal*). What does she know of my hands? She couldn't imagine where these hands have been.

DOCTOR. I'm not supposed to know who you are, that's what Semyon Pavlovitch wants, but then, he does nothing to hide it, lets a phrase slip, so that it becomes obvious.

MARIA LVOVNA (*internal*). It's like the informers they send to sit at your table in a restaurant, taking notes while you discuss the menu. It's their way of showing contempt for human intelligence.

DOCTOR. I have to go along with it, but I did want you to know, Madame Dzerzinskaya, that I know. Perhaps it will make you trust me.

MARIA LVOVNA (*internal*). You never. That boy, perhaps; he's not ambitious. But what does it matter whom I trust anymore? Once I gave it to everyone, even total strangers, pretending to be interested in my opinion about this or that musician, or my view of Georgian national folk dance ensembles. I never turned them away, even after my flat was ransacked, after the vulgar telephone calls, even after some harmless remark to one of them – who knows, perhaps it happened that way? – condemned me.

Fades into birds singing outside open window.

MIKHAIL (*breathing deep*). Listen, Pavel Ilyitch. Can you hear them?

PAVEL. The taxis?

MIKHAIL. The birds. The dawn chorus. I can't remember the last time I heard them. Every night, just after the 'Internationale', I drive home and eat the warmed-up slops my old mother has left for me, and settle down to a night of insomnia. But even then, I don't hear the birds where I live, ever since I was forced to take my mother in.

PAVEL. Perhaps they come to eat crusts and lay their eggs there. They just don't sing anymore, in your district, Mikhail Karlovitch.

MIKHAIL (*secretive*). Do you think *he* hears them? There in his dacha?

PAVEL. No doubt.

MIKHAIL. Already? It's only just gone five o'clock.

PAVEL. They're louder in the country.

MIKHAIL. Perhaps he hears them and is already stirring. What do you think he'll have for breakfast this morning?

PAVEL. This doesn't concern me.

MIKHAIL. It concerns all of us.

Fade in uncontrolled breathing and sniffling of Maria Lvovna, and sound of drip switch.

DOCTOR. I read about your case, I followed it every day in the newspaper, and we discussed it in study groups at Party Youth headquarters. The question was raised: how could someone like that, with her background, with her privileges, with all public doors open to her, how could she betray the trust placed in her? And I answered: perhaps she didn't. I can still remember the careful silence that followed. I had dared to say what the others only allowed themselves to think. And then, some nights later, the end of your trial was broadcast on the radio. It was prefaced by one of your recordings, which I found strange because, for some months already, these were no longer played. I thought: this is a sign that they will let her go free. Then came your voice before the court, admitting everything you had done, the entire disgusting catalogue, in the most sickening detail, so that it could not have been invented. I will never forgive you, Maria Lvovna, for having been found guilty.

Scene 15
Piano plays beginning of third movement. Played better. It is played throughout the trial sequence. Maria Lvovna's physical effort in playing can also be heard through vocal exclamations. Occasionally, she sings or hums briefly to the music.

PROSECUTOR (*after a time*). Accused Dzerzinskaya, what is your profession?

MARIA LVOVNA. That is well known to the court.

PROSECUTOR. Do you know the composer Rykowski?

MARIA LVOVNA. I have worked with him.

PROSECUTOR. To overthrow the government?

MARIA LVOVNA. To perform his Piano Concerto.

PROSECUTOR. Do you wish to take the court back to the shameful days of the opening of this trial, when you denied the charges against you?

MARIA LVOVNA. I declare that I am willing to work with the court in finding me guilty of the crimes listed in the indictment. But I do not wish to implicate others.

PROSECUTOR. You are trying to convince the court that you were not part of Rykowski's terrorist group?

MARIA LVOVNA. I only played his Piano Concerto.

PROSECUTOR. Rykowski has testified that coded messages were passed in the hollowed-out parts of a tuba during orchestra rehearsals. Why not also under the lid of a grand piano?

Piano plays. Fifteen seconds.

And then?

MARIA LVOVNA (*monotone*). Rykowski asked me to consider a trip to Vienna . . .

PROSECUTOR. Under the guise of a concert tour?

MARIA LVOVNA. Under the skies of a concert tour, so we could meet Western agents . . .

PROSECUTOR. Just a moment. You said: 'Under the skies of a concert tour.' What does that mean?

MARIA LVOVNA (*frightened*). Mean?

PROSECUTOR. You know what meaning means?

MARIA LVOVNA (*confused*). I . . .

PROSECUTOR. Why did you not accompany Rykowski to Vienna?

MARIA LVOVNA. I was unable.

PROSECUTOR. Unable?

MARIA LVOVNA. For personal reasons.

PROSECUTOR. But you would have done so if you could?

MARIA LVOVNA. Yes, I . . .

PROSECUTOR. To what end?

MARIA LVOVNA. To help him in his plans to meet members of the . . . the . . .

PROSECUTOR. The Trotskyist Opposition.

MARIA LVOVNA. The Trotskyist Opposition and also Austrian agents working for them. I could speak German and Rykowski not.

PROSECUTOR. What was the purpose of your speaking German?

MARIA LVOVNA. For my work.

PROSECUTOR. Passing coded messages? What are the names of these Germans you worked with?

MARIA LVOVNA. Bach, Brahms, Schumann . . .

Harsh piano chord. Maria Lvovna screams externally.

Scene 16

SEMYON (*speaking on the telephone*). Yes, that's what I said: all traffic west out of Moscow is to be halted between eight and nine o'clock this morning for . . . On whose orders? Mine. I'm sending a limousine to Secretary Stalin, who needs an order, cretin? No, there will be no written request. You will simply clear a path from the central Moscow radio station to the Western road, so that the limousine may pass at top speed without encountering any obstacles . . . What is your name, Comrade? Ulkov, Good, I've noted that down. Now, Ulkov, let me speak to your superior. I don't care if he's sleeping. I'm also sleeping. I'll wait, yes, but not for long. The chauffeur, Mikhail Karlovitch, have you alerted him?

MIKHAIL. He's been sleeping in the car for hours. Everyone's ready. Except Maria Lvovna.

SEMYON. The Doctor's trying to calm her down.

MIKHAIL. And me? Who will calm me down? Who is thinking of me?

SEMYON. We're all thinking of you. Otherwise we wouldn't be here.

MIKHAIL. That's easily said. With every hour that passes, I find myself drifting from job to job, clearing canals in the countryside, then taking to begging for soup at farmhouse windows, at last being warned by passers-by that they are coming for me, that a cell is being disinfected for my use, and that members of the First State Firing Squad are being recalled from their holiday spas.

SEMYON. I'm also risking everything, just being in your vicinity.

MIKHAIL. Only because you've burned your bridges, Semyon Pavlovitch, insulted and alienated everyone who could possibly owe you a favour. Now I am in your debt and, knowing you, you'll milk me dry before you are satisfied.

SEMYON. What could you possibly do for me?

MIKHAIL. Some of your young lady protégées might give anything to be heard on the radio.

SEMYON. They already give anything just to have me accept them into the Musicians' Union. You'd have to do better than that.

MIKHAIL. I might dust off some archive recordings in which you conduct the orchestra, those no one has wanted to listen to for years, so that you could claim royalties . . .

SEMYON. This is half a radish to a starving man. Are you trying to make a fool of me? (*Telephone.*) What's that? You again, Ulkov? Where is your superior? He says to call back in the afternoon. Fine. This has all been noted down. I hope you aren't claustrophobic, Ulkov. I understand it's very close work mining salt. (*Hangs up.*) So much for the Traffic Bureau. Shall I call the police directly?

MIKHAIL. The station chauffeur is himself a secret policeman. Let him arrange it.

SEMYON. Don't forget to tell him.

PAVEL. The Doctor is signalling you from the Studio, Semyon Pavlovitch.

SEMYON. Switch on her microphone. . . . I can hear you now, Sophia Ivanovna.

DOCTOR (*from Studio, heard in Control Room*). She is completely broken down. This has all been too hard for her. She's trembling . . .

SEMYON. So are we all, Doctor. Just get on with your job. We have to finish the recording.

DOCTOR. What do you expect me to do?

SEMYON. Whatever is necessary.

DOCTOR. No more injections. The human body can only take so much.

SEMYON. Her body is no longer human, Doctor. It has already gone beyond its threshold. We're talking about one last half hour in a long and rich life. Surely it is in your power to give us this.

DOCTOR. She is indicating that she wants to sleep.

SEMYON. So do we all. . . . Dear Maria Lvovna, we're appealing to you from the Control Room: you are halfway through the third and final movement. You have already worked miracles tonight. Back on form, just as you were before you took time off from the rigours of concert touring. We in here have given up our sleep for you tonight, our wives and Mikhail Karlovitch's mother are all wondering where we are. What are we sacrificing our time and energy for, if not so that you can be revered again as you deserve?

Chair moved noisily in Control Room.

MIKHAIL. Where are you going, Pavel Ilyitch?

PAVEL. To be sick.

MIKHAIL. Make it brief. It's ten past six.

SEMYON. How long will it take a shot of cortisone to work, Doctor?

DOCTOR. Twenty minutes, but . . .

SEMYON. Good. We start again at six thirty.

Scene 17
With piano in studio. Trial sequence internal. Snatches of 'Sous les Toits de Paris', irregular breathing of Maria Lvovna, then:

MARIA LVOVNA (*normal voice*). Before the court I plead guilty to all the crimes mentioned in the indictment against me, which have brought shame upon my life. Before the court I also declare and underline and repeat now, that I plead guilty for the entire block of criminals led by myself and Rykowski. I demand of the court the highest penalty, and I agree with the State Prosecutor, who has repeated here several times that I stand perhaps at the threshold of my death. My criminal character should be obvious to all who see . . . what? Radio? . . . to all who hear my voice today, my political guilt is boundless, my legal responsibility is such that only the severest judgment will suffice. Even that would not be enough, for I deserve to be shot ten times over.

Scene 18
Piano heard in control room, played well. Drinking, but no drunkenness.

MIKHAIL (*drinking*). It used to be said of her: just sit her in front of a piano and the rest of life passes into the background.

SEMYON (*drinking*). You know, Doctor, watching her there in her wheelchair, moving that feeding tube along the piano, those splints keeping the knuckles at right angles, I have the feeling of watching a marionette you've set in motion. As if the sound . . . even the sound she makes has been injected into her by your syringes, free of human effort. If we are on the edge of success at this moment, we owe it all to you, Sophia Ivanovna, by way of this artificial masterpiece you've constructed there in the Studio.

DOCTOR. This is a human being, Semyon Pavlovitch.

SEMYON. Nothing human could have achieved what she has tonight. No, Doctor, *I'm* a human being, incapable of even slouching through a single day without drawing the contempt of everyone who passes in the street.

DOCTOR. She has had to suffer to do what she did tonight.

SEMYON. Spare your sympathy. She is beyond feeling now. What we're hearing is pure reflex.

MIKHAIL. It sounds like the old Dzerzinskaya to me. Almost.

SEMYON. No. This is only the clay model reconstructed from her remains.

PAVEL. I've heard enough. You don't know what it means to have the will to stay alive.

SEMYON. There is no will there, Pavel Ilyitch. Only cortisone.

PAVEL (*chair*). I'm leaving.

A switch is thrown and we hear the rest of the scene in the studio, that is, with Maria Lvovna.

MIKHAIL. Not until the sonata finishes.

PAVEL. It's finished for me.

MIKHAIL. You must still press the record.

PAVEL. Do it yourself.

MIKHAIL. Do you know what you are saying?

SEMYON. Let him go, Mikhail Karlovitch. We've seen them before, sparkling boys like him with . . . what do you call them? . . . principles, swaggering bright-eyed into a world that covers them in spit. It won't last long, his sense of outrage. Or he won't. One or the other.

PAVEL. No one is disposable, Semyon Pavlovitch.

SEMYON. You are.

PAVEL. It's Mikhail Karlovitch's decision whether I return here tomorrow, not yours.

SEMYON. If you leave here now, before this record is pressed, so that Secretary Stalin can have it for breakfast in his melancholy mood, then Mikhail Karlovitch will not be here tomorrow to decide even what's for lunch.

DOCTOR. For Secretary Stalin?

SEMYON. Yes, Doctor.

MARIA LVOVNA (*internal*). 'Stalin'.

DOCTOR. I thought it was to launch Maria Lvovna on a new career.

SEMYON. No. It is to gratify a curious whim of our Party Leader. But this is not something I want her to know before she has finished the sonata.

DOCTOR. Why not?

SEMYON. She would not understand.

MARIA LVOVNA (*internal*). 'Stalin!'

DOCTOR. Who would not be honoured to make a recording for him?

Throat clearing on microphone. Sonata slows down. She suddenly plays some bars of honky-tonk, which turn into thunderous chords, then pure noise, then stops.

Scene 19
In studio.

SEMYON. Where are you running in that wheelchair?

DOCTOR. She's pulled out the drip-pin!

SEMYON. Don't make us chase you round the Studio, Maria Lvovna. Where has she got the energy from? Come back here. Trap her in the corner. Step on the brake behind the chair.

Violent protest from Maria Lvovna.

DOCTOR. Hold her please, Semyon Pavlovitch. I need to take her pulse.

SEMYON. Maria Lvovna, we're down to the last three minutes. If it's food you want, I promise you a hot breakfast. After the work is done. If you're tired, we'll organise a first-class hotel.

DOCTOR. Two hours ago I couldn't find her pulse. Now it's racing madly.

Mikhail Karlovitch and Pavel Ilyitch can be heard talking in Control Room through loud speaker in Studio.

SEMYON. Maria Lvovna . . . No, don't pull away from me. It's seven-thirty in the morning and we have a deadline to fulfill. You can't just stop before the end. You were doing . . . fine . . . approaching the shadow of the years before your prime. I was almost proud of you . . .

Conversation in Control Room loud.

Can you please switch off the microphone so I can think, Mikhail Karlovitch?

MIKHAIL (*from Control Room*). What microphone?

SEMYON. I can hear everything you say in there.

MIKHAIL. Why is it on? It shouldn't be live while we're recording.

PAVEL. I switched it on.

MIKHAIL. Why?

PAVEL. So that Maria Lvovna could hear what you were saying.

Silence.

MIKHAIL (*gasping*). Semyon Pavlovitch!

SEMYON. Yes. That's it. She knows.

Scene 20
Semyon Pavlovitch smoking. Breathing of Maria Lvovna.

SEMYON (*after a time, softly at first*). I didn't know you were still alive until I heard it from the Minister of Culture. I never imagined you'd survive two years of prison. Not fragile you.

MARIA LVOVNA (*internal*). He smokes to kill me. He knows I never allowed it.

SEMYON. I thought: to see her again, to hear her play, however poorly, was worth a sleepless night. And for you, a chance to sit at the piano again, even for one last brief night of your life . . . you couldn't have hoped for that two years ago.

MIKHAIL (*from Control Room*). Semyon Pavlovitch . . .

SEMYON. Tell me what you want, Maria Lvovna. Anything. It doesn't matter. Finish the sonata, and I'll take you for a carriage ride through the park like the times you grew bored with your husband, and no longer cared about being discreet. I'll take you there on your way back to prison.

MARIA LVOVNA (*internal, frightened*). Prison? No, it can't be . . .

SEMYON. Why are you staring? Where did you think you were going? We brought you here to play music. Prove to me you've earned some other fate.

MARIA LVOVNA (*internal*). Just to frighten me. Why would they send me back after letting me out? Black is white, I know that trick.

Click of brake, wheelchair rolled.

SEMYON. Now. These are your hands. This is a piano. He calls out to you. You could never resist him. Your back grows weak and your fingers long for him. Reach out and stroke him.

Dark, minor chords.

SEMYON. Fool. Spare me your resistance. It's a false luxury at this late hour. The time for it was two years ago. Maybe. Now, it's absurd. There's nothing left for you, broken, hollow woman. These heroics bore me to death before I've had my morning coffee. It's not worthy of you. Three minutes more Mozart and you can disappear without trace. This is the least I can expect of you.

MARIA LVOVNA (*internal*). This is not his voice. His throat has been re-educated, all the old cadences and rhythms are gone from it.

SEMYON. I'm waiting for you to say something.

MARIA LVOVNA (*internal*). Silence keeps my voice clean.

SEMYON. Why don't you speak? They didn't pull out your tongue. Why this contempt?

MARIA LVOVNA (*internal*). You are one they didn't have to break physically, Semyon. They simply poisoned you with cynicism. What kind of child would ours have been?

SEMYON. What is it you want, Masya? Shall I apologise? Does it really matter to you? And would you believe me anyway? I had no choice but to give evidence. You deserved it anyway. You knew that every remark was taken down. I can't even remember what it is you were supposed to have said. But somehow, it seems, it might have got back to him . . . to . . . (*Whispers.*) Stalin . . . and he might have taken it personally, as an attack on his taste in music, something like that, who can remember, and what does it matter now? It wasn't my lies that set you up, they had it all invented already, in your dossier, what they needed against you, I just said yes. And, to tell you the truth, I owe my position as Chief of the Musician's Union to my cooperation in the case against you, and it meant I was able to help young musicians get a start in life. So, after all, some good has come out of it.

Silence.

I'm running out of patience, Maria Lvovna. You are going to finish that sonata, if I have to break your fingers all over again. It would be wiser to demand something of me.

MARIA LVOVNA (*internally*). Yes.

SEMYON. Some Belgian chocolates you used to like. I can get them on the black market and have them sent to you in prison.

MARIA LVOVNA (*internal*). Prison.

SEMYON. I've had enough of this. I'll call the chauffeur to bring you back.

MARIA LVOVNA (*internal*). No! Wait!

Piano plays Chopin Mazurka.

SEMYON. This is Chopin, not Mozart.

Chopin continues.

SEMYON. You played this as an encore in Prague the time I followed you there.

Semyon bangs the piano with fist.

SEMYON. I'd rather die by firing squad than have you jog my memories of good times.

Piano plays 'Sous les Toits de Paris'.

SEMYON. What's this? You want to work in that café again? I risked my life to get you that job there three years ago. What do you think would happen to me now?

MARIA LVOVNA (*internal, frustrated*). No, no.

Plays Chopin.

SEMYON. I said no Chopin!

Piano plays 'Sous les Toits de Paris'.

MIKHAIL (*through microphone*). Semyon Pavlovitch, it's nearly eight o'clock!

SEMYON. Quiet! She's trying to tell me something.

'Sous les Toits de Paris' more insistent.

SEMYON. What is it? You want to work again . . .

Harsh chords. Then 'Sous les Toits de Paris'.

MARIA LVOVNA (*internal*). No, no, no!

SEMYON. If not that, what then?

'Sous les Toits de Paris'.

SEMYON (*singing to himself*). . . . (*pauses.*) Paris. (*Silence, then softly.*) Out of the question.

Insistent 'Sous les Toits de Paris'.

SEMYON. For a start. I don't have that much influence, Masya.

'London Bridge'.

SEMYON. No.

'On the Road to Mandalay'.

SEMYON. London, Mandalay, Paris, it's all the same. You won't be allowed to leave the country. Don't ask it of me. Anything else.

'Tales from the Vienna Woods'.

SEMYON. Look. In the Ukraine there's a work camp. It's a very mild regime. You'd only have to stuff pillows with goose feathers. It's a long day and the food is abysmal, but you'd be less bored than where you are now. I had my brother sent there after he'd been sentenced to twelve years hard labour. I risked everything to get him better settled. I promise you . . .

MARIA LVOVNA (*internal*). No, never.

SEMYON. . . . that I'll do all in my power to see if they have a place free, a spare mattress. You'd have to be registered under an assumed name, and we would say that you'd died in prison. After all, it's almost true and nobody noticed it, no one would have noticed if . . .

'London Bridge'.

SEMYON. No. In the Ukraine I can hide you away. But . . . free, elsewhere in the world . . . Sooner or later, you'd recover, you'd turn up again. You might give a concert somewhere . . . in Prague or Paris or London and . . . he . . . Sta . . . The Party First Secretary . . . might just hear about it. Look, I'm offering you something, Masya, take it. This Mikhail Karlovitch, if he fails to deliver your recording this morning, he goes down and he'll drag me with him.

Chopin played. Violent slaps. Maria Lvovna crying.

DOCTOR (*entering studio*). Semyon Pavlovitch!

SEMYON. I'm not a violent man, Sophia Ivanovna. Please don't get the impression that I strike women, a man of my background, in my day we were taught to revere our mothers. She has done this to me, this once-was-a-woman-thing here, she has provoked a peaceful man like me to outrage.

DOCTOR. You have knocked out a tooth.

SEMYON. She'll hardly miss it on a prison diet.

Maria Lvovna crying.

Escort her to the police van waiting outside, Doctor. I promised to have her back in her quarters before daybreak.

MIKHAIL. Are you mad? She hasn't finished the sonata!

SEMYON. And won't, Mikhail Karlovitch, no matter how much you beg. I've seen her like this before, puffed up with false pride, standing fast by something she thinks is worthy of defending. You'd think this would have been twisted out of her by now. But no. It comes from her fanatical dedication to music.

MIKHAIL. What will I do now?

SEMYON. You used to be a musician, Mikhail Karlovitch.

MIKHAIL. Me? I played the cello when I was a student.

SEMYON. At least you can read music.

MIKHAIL. You mean, I should finish the sonata myself?

SEMYON. Who else?

MIKHAIL. And Pavel Ilyitch has walked out on us. Who will cut the disc?

SEMYON. The Doctor here.

DOCTOR. I don't know anything about it.

SEMYON. Imagine you're wielding a scalpel.

MIKHAIL. This is impossible.

SEMYON. It's eight o'clock. He'll be shaving by now.

Scene 21
Throughout speech, fading in and out of applause, peppered with
'bravos', 'encore' etc. Constant sound of car motor, moving through
traffic.

MARIA LVOVNA (*internal*). I want no thanks for it, I've earned no
applause, I want to sleep, but my head keeps bumping as we ride over
cobblestones, I was almost there, almost asleep, and then I heard the
applause and the cries for an encore. Almost there, on the outskirts
of where things have to be remembered, but the applause kept rising
in me like a sickness, let it be over, let it be over, the music. Lift
your head. One last time. To the window. Daylight. At the end of
this Boulevard is the train station. At nine-fifteen, every day, for
many years, you could get the sleeper to Prague. You closed your
eyes and you were there. They let you sleep then. Driver, carry my
suitcase to compartment thirty-two.

Scene 22
The last bars of the sonata, played hesitantly, very badly. Finishes.
Cynical clapping from the control room. Mikhail Karlovitch weeping
on piano.

SEMYON. You'll need to edit out his whimpering, Doctor.

EATING WORDS

by Richard Nelson

For Ned Chaillet

Richard Nelson is the author of two other radio plays, *Languages Spoken Here* (Radio 3, Giles Cooper Award, 1987) and *Roots in Water* (Radio 3, 1989). His stage plays include *Some Americans Abroad* (Royal Shakespeare Company, Lincoln Center Theatre Company, New York), *Principia Scriptoriae* (RSC, Manhattan Theatre Club, New York), *Between East and West* (Hampstead), as well as *The Vienna Notes*, *Rip Van Winkle or the Works*, *An American Comedy*, and *The Return of Pinocchio* which have been produced by many theatres in the United States. He is the author of numerous adaptations and translations which have been seen at theatres across the United States and on Broadway, and he wrote the book for the Broadway production of the musical, *Chess*. Richard Nelson has won many awards, including two OBIEs, a 1987 *Time Out* Award, a Guggenheim Fellowship and the 1986 ABC Television Playwriting Award. His television plays include *Sensibility and Sense* and *The End of a Sentence* (both American Playhouse, Public TV, US). In September his new play, *Two Shakespearean Actors*, will be performed by the RSC in the Swan Theatre, Stratford.

Eating Words was first broadcast as part of the Globe Theatre Season, on BBC Radio 4/World Service on 30 October 1989. The cast was as follows:

HENRY – an English writer in his fifties	John Woodvine
VANESSA – his older sister	Sheila Allen
SAM – an American writer in his fifties	Ed Asner
YOUNG WOMAN IN PUB	Emily Richard
WAITER	Charles Simpson
PEOPLE IN RESTAURANT AND PUB	Vincent Brimble
	John Bull
	David King
	Elizabeth Mansfield
PEOPLE IN PUB	Simon Treves
	Joe Dunlop
	Christopher Good
	Danny Schiller

Director: Ned Chaillet
Running time, as broadcast: approximately 65 minutes

Scene 1
HENRY AND SAM GET TOGETHER TWICE A YEAR FOR LUNCH.

A posh restaurant in the West End, London. Lunchtime. HENRY, fifties, and his sister, VANESSA, early sixties, sit waiting.

VANESSA. You've read his book, haven't you? The new one. It's out.

Beat.

I saw it in Waterstone's. It's in the window.

Beat.

I suppose it shall do very well.

Beat.

Being in the window. (*Short pause.*) He's going to ask what you think about his book you know.

HENRY. No he won't. He's cleverer than that. (*Reaching for the wine bottle.*) You are sure you don't want a drink? It might make the play –

VANESSA. I'd fall asleep, Henry. I shall probably fall asleep anyway, but . . . (*Laughs.*) Theatre has become so . . .

HENRY. Hasn't it. (*Pouring the wine.*) But you don't mind if I –

VANESSA. Drink what you like, Henry, I'm not counting.

HENRY. Can I do nothing wrong?

Beat.

I should be ill more often.

VANESSA. You are not ill.

Beat.

You are not ill, you are getting better.

HENRY. And if I don't – you'll kill me. (*Laughs.*) Here he is now.

SAM, *early fifties, American, approaches their table.*

SAM (*sitting down*). Sorry I'm late. I waited forever for a tube. I hope you haven't –

HENRY. No. No. Sit down. Excuse me for not getting up.

VANESSA. Henry –

HENRY. You've met my sister, Vanessa, haven't you?

SAM. I'm sure we –

VANESSA. With your wife.

HENRY. Hand me your glass.

VANESSA. What an actress. Henry, that's what I was starting to say – what the theatre is missing. She should never have left the stage.

SAM. My wife still acts. She hasn't left –

VANESSA (*not hearing*). She is missed! Sorely missed. Tell her that for me, will you?

SAM. Actually, she's in a play right –

VANESSA (*not hearing*). What time is it, dear?

HENRY. You'd better go.

SAM. Go? How late am – ?

HENRY. Vanessa just dropped me off. She's seeing –

VANESSA. Do excuse me for running like this, but you know the theatre, it waits for no one. (*Goes to kiss Henry.*) I'll pick you up, Henry. Now what theatre was it again?

HENRY. The Phoenix.

VANESSA. Yes.

Beat.

Yes. That is the one. Sam.

SAM. Vanessa.

VANESSA. Now just don't take your wife away to America. We need her here, Sam. Don't do like you did with poor Richard Burton.

She leaves.

SAM. What did I do to Richard Burton?

Short pause.

HENRY (*as he drinks*). She's seeing the matinee of the Tom Howard play.

SAM. Lucky her.

HENRY. Say that again.

Beat.

SAM. What? I just said –

HENRY. And I said she's seeing the *Tom Howard*. And then you said – lucky her.

SAM. So?

Beat.

What's wrong with – ?

HENRY. The last time we talked about Howard –

SAM. I trashed him, I remember this.

Beat.

And – this may come as a surprise to you, Henry, but later I felt quite terrible about what I'd said. I mean, I for one think we should try to be a little more generous to our peers. It isn't an easy thing – writing – we both know that. So why every writer feels the need, almost the obsession, to attack his contemporaries, this I do not know.

Beat.

And this, I have decided to do something about.

Beat.

I have vowed that if I do not have something positive to say about a fellow writer then I shall say nothing at all.

HENRY. And this goes for Tom Howard?

SAM. My lips are sealed.

They laugh.

HENRY. I believed you there for a second.

SAM. No you didn't.

HENRY. Really, I was beginning to worry that I was going to have to watch what I said.

SAM. Bullshit. When have we ever watched what we said. How long have we been having these lunches –

HENRY. I thought –

SAM. Years, right. I don't remember exactly, but years. And when have we ever watched what we said.

Beat.

And after three bottles of wine, when have we ever remembered what we said.

He laughs. HENRY *laughs.*

SAM. Speaking of –

HENRY. I'll get another bottle. Chardonnay is fine? You know I can't drink red –

SAM. I'm drinking it, aren't I? So don't ask.

Short pause.

Which is our's, the guy or the girl?

HENRY. It's a guy, but not him.

SAM. A guy though. So that's what I get for being late.

HENRY. I think he's just assigned to this –

SAM. I was just joking. I didn't mean –

HENRY. Oh. I –

Beat.

That's him.

Beat.

He sees me.

Pause.

HENRY. So . . .

Beat.

Come on, do I look that bad?

SAM. What do you mean? You look –

HENRY. At least I'm not dead yet.

Beat.

Vanessa is taking very good care of me. So I am assured of a slow death. (*Laughs.*)

SAM. You look terrific. Really. You do.

Short pause.

HENRY. Thank you.

SAM. Now who was it that said you'd been looking ill? Somebody was saying that. I'll have to remember who it was and put him straight. You look terrific. (*Pause.*) Have you looked over the menu?

Beat.

Give me a second then.

Pause.

HENRY. Your new book is out.

SAM. Uh-huh.

Beat.

Have you seen the jacket? It looks like someone threw up on a book.

Beat.

HENRY. That should do a lot for sales.

SAM. Tell me about it.

Pause. Fade out begins.

SAM. What are you having?

HENRY. The fish here is usually . . .

Fade out.

Scene 2
SAM'S ADVENTURE OF THE NEW BOOK.

The restaurant. HENRY and SAM are eating their main courses.

SAM. I told her that every writer uses what's around him. Where else does he look?

Beat.

You were right about the salmon.

HENRY. I have never had bad fish here.

SAM. It's a good place to know about.

HENRY. Especially in the West End.

SAM. There's so many –

HENRY. Aren't there. That's why this place is good to know.

SAM. Funny, I think I've passed it. I don't know. It's been here for a while?

HENRY. A couple of years at least.

SAM. Amazing.

Beat.

Anyway . . .

HENRY (*eating*). Back to Mary.

SAM. And it's not *just* Mary. I'm telling you this has gotten serious.

Beat.

Look, I will admit to maybe having been a tiny bit bald about taking from . . . using . . . no, it wasn't 'using'. As I have been saying, where else does a writer look for his ideas? 'Using' sounds like 'stealing' or something. Plagiarising, even.

Beat.

So – I quote unquote took from people we know. But I have always done that; after twelve novels you would think Mary would understand that.

Beat.

I *need* to take it from wherever I can get it.

Beat.

The stories were just sitting there to incorporate.

Beat.

I observe life. This is what we do, Henry. That is how I see it.

Short pause.

And Ben's going to college next year. You can't afford to start getting picky.

HENRY (*eating*). Mary mentioned that. It doesn't seem possible.

SAM. How long did you and Mary talk anyway?

HENRY. We just –

SAM. Forget it. She's called everyone. You'd think I'd committed some sort of heinous crime against nature.

Beat.

She married me, after all.

Short pause.

Look, I don't want to bore –

HENRY. No, please. I've been wanting to hear about what's been going on ever since she phoned –

SAM. She must have thought that because we were having lunch –

HENRY. She didn't mention our having lunch.

SAM. No?

Beat.

She's told everyone, I'm sure. Hell.

Short pause.

HENRY. I think she called to see how I was doing.

SAM. Of course she did.

Pause.

Henry, I'm sorry; why I'm –

HENRY. She said Ben wants to go to school in the States.

SAM. Yeh. I don't know why. He'd done the work for Oxford. Do you know why? Did Mary – ?

HENRY. No. No, she didn't say.

Short pause.

SAM. She doesn't talk to me.

HENRY. I gathered. But you can't tell me this is the first time you've used your wife in a story.

SAM. Of course it's not!

Beat.

Of course. (*Laughs.*) And that is my goddamn point, Henry! A million times before. Maybe not so . . . so . . . I don't know, blatant. For chrissake even her mother calls from Ohio. So how the hell did she get a copy? Knopf doesn't even publish until the end of the month.

HENRY. How did she?

SAM (*realising*). Mary sent her bound galleys. That's how!

HENRY. Or maybe the legal department at Knopf, if she's somebody –

SAM. My mother-in-law is nobody. Nobody knows her. Even if she was the character in the bloody book which I am not saying she is, nobody's ever going to know it.

Beat.

And I do not make fun. I *have* fun with this character. You understand that.

HENRY. Sure.

Short pause.

SAM. Mary. Maybe one or two of her sisters, *maybe* I put them into the book – as characters. A few things that have happened to them, I have *incorporated*. Or rather, I have *recorded*. But I twist these around and use them for my purposes, Henry. I am a writer, after all. I am a novelist. Do they not know this? Do they not realise that this is what I do?

Beat.

Okay maybe, and just maybe, they are recognisable to one or two close friends, or family members or maybe a few other people around the town they live in. So what is the big deal? I would be honoured.

Beat.

And as for her father, he's dead for chrissake. What *is* the big deal? He can't be offended.

Beat.

Him I admit using. Not the mother. Only the father.

HENRY. And he's dead.

SAM. That is right.

Beat.

But I don't use his name. I change some things.

Beat.

Why am I on the defensive anyway? That is the question. This is art after all. And you take things from life! And it is in this way – this is what I should have said to her – this is how food has been put on the table for the last twenty-two years. This is how she has been able to keep *her* artistic integrity working only on plays that quote unquote matter to her, and pay about two pence. What does she think I've been doing all these years, writing goddamn fairy tales?!!

Short pause.

HENRY. I say we start on another bottle, don't you?

SAM. I'm not writing today. So why not get plastered.

Pours.

HENRY. Cheers.

SAM. Cheers.

HENRY. Anyway, Sam – to your book. May you have a success despite everything.

SAM. Thanks.

They drink.

And to your health, Henry.

HENRY. Despite everything.

They drink. Awkward pause.

SAM. Sorry, I keep bumping –

HENRY. These wheelchairs are built rather clunky. I could turn to the side –

SAM. Please, no. No. Henry, I wasn't saying . . .

Beat.

My fault really.

Short pause.

HENRY. It doesn't embarrass me anymore, Sam.

SAM. Why should it ever have?

Beat.

Anyway about my book . . .

HENRY. To change the subject.

SAM. That was the subject one minute ago, Henry.

Beat.

So – you should have seen the jacket design I wanted. There's this friend of mine, a wonderful designer. He would have done it as a favour really. Books pay nothing compared to . . . I don't know. Other stuff. Business-type stuff. He told me what he had in mind. It was great. But Anton said no. I think it sounded too inviting, the idea, and god forbid a book should look inviting.

Beat.

What publishers know about publishing.

HENRY. You could write on the head of a –

SAM. You want to know what sort of publicity they're giving me? Anton's all hot about this. They are buying a quarter page ad in the *Times Supplement.*

Beat.

When he told me you'd have thought he was handing over a million pounds.

HENRY. Why don't you move?

SAM. Because I'm loyal!!

Beat.

And because everybody's no different. It's bad in New York, but here . . . I shouldn't be surprised. I know what to expect: the moment I first walked into Anton's office – Anton's closet would be more appropriate – whatever they call the place where his publisher keeps Anton, and there on his desk was a manual typewriter. Not a wordprocessor, not an electronic typewriter, not even a goddamn electric. A manual that looks like he'd been given it when he went off to boarding school.

HENRY. Probably was.

SAM. You write. You work. You struggle. And you end up like dust collecting on a shelf.

HENRY. Are you talking about Anton or – ?

SAM. You are supposed to feel good. The book comes out, you have something in your hands that you can touch, that takes up space and you should feel pretty satisfied. At least for a moment or two.

HENRY. It's going to do very well. It's going to be a smash.

SAM. I tell Mary that and she cries. She says she's never going to tell me another secret for as long as she lives. I ask her: what secrets have you told me? I don't remember one secret she's ever told me.

HENRY. She'll get over it. Once you get the reviews. She'll see.

SAM. The first one was OK.

HENRY. You've already been –

SAM. Two.

Beat.

Just two. The first – they got Fred to do it. And Fred has always been good to me. He likes me.

Beat.

I like him.

HENRY. He's a jerk.

SAM. Not to me.

Beat.

But it was that asshole on the *Observer* –

HENRY. I missed that. When did –

SAM. Next week.

Beat.

If critics knew what they did.

Beat.

What they let loose.

Beat.

This scumbag starts talking about the wife – right from the beginning he is obsessed with the wife character. He says she's pathetic. In this age of liberation, he takes her apart. Mary needs no more ammunition than that.

Short pause.

It's not just the reader who reads these things. It's us. We read them.

Beat.

We read them with our kids around us running and playing – when my kids still ran and played – I do remember this – it used to be really savage. Ben used to cry – 'Daddy's got *another* bad review!'

Beat.

Of course then I'd have to say – 'But Ben, it is not all bad, this gentleman does say a few rather OK things about your Dad's new novel on which he has slaved these past two years. Or rather, Ben, it is the things he has chosen not to say that should give us heart.' Like – that he didn't throw up reading it and rip it up and flush it down the toilet.

Short pause.

So – the *Observer*. Thank you, thank you, thank you.

Pause.

HENRY. Maybe Mary won't –

SAM. A friend – a quote unquote friend – has already sent a copy to her. She works at this newspaper.

Beat.

Yesterday morning, at 10 am, she sent it. I guess she figured she could destroy my whole day that way. Plus of course THE MOTHER phones as well with her unsolicited review.

Beat.

It is something like six in the morning in Cleveland and she has been up all night reading and crying over my book – and there is not a lot in it that should be sad, Henry.

Beat.

Yesterday was fun; what a fun fun day it was.

Beat.

I have a deal with myself not to have a drink before six-thirty, do you do that?

HENRY. I used to.

SAM. Except for lunches like this.

HENRY. Because you're not writing.

SAM. Right.

Short pause.

That rule almost broke me yesterday.

HENRY. I'm sorry.

Pause.

SAM (*sighs, takes a sip of wine*). Anyway, I hear the *Guardian*'s going to be positive. Maybe even better than that; Anton's heard about it, but hasn't seen it, so I think he's being quite cautious with me.

Beat.

We'll see.

HENRY. I'm sure it'll be –

SAM. It better.

Beat.

Please, please, please.

Pause as they eat.

HENRY (*finally*). About Mary's reaction to seeing a character based on herself –

SAM. A couple of similarities. And the wife isn't the jerk! I'm the jerk.

Beat.

The husband in the book is the jerk.

HENRY. Right.

Short pause.

I was going to say that I have had a somewhat similar experience; with Keith and my book, *The Lefthander*.

SAM. Oh yes.

HENRY. You've read it?

SAM. Everyone thinks it's your best book. I love that sort of thing.

HENRY. I wouldn't think it was –

Beat.

So I watched Keith as he read it. I had given him the proofs. I made lunch for us and watched this black gay guy reading my book about this big black gay guy and his –

Beat.

Well, you've read the book, right?

Beat.

It sold like nothing.

SAM. That's not what I heard.

HENRY. It's being re-issued with a series of gay novels. Anyway, when Keith finished it, you know what he said?

Beat.

He said. 'Remember what happened to Joe Orton.'

Beat.

That's it.

Beat.

I still published the book. And Keith forgot about it I guess. Or maybe he even ended up a little flattered. Who knows. (*Laughs to himself.*)

SAM. But what you're saying is that you thought Keith was really threatening – ?

HENRY. I think he was joking.

Beat.

The character as you may remember isn't a bad character.

SAM. Neither is the mother-in-law in my book, Henry!

Beat.

A bit silly maybe, but if you listen to Mary and her sisters talk about their mother – If I put that sort of thing in – What I wrote doesn't – That family should be thanking me. That is what I think.

Short pause.

Orton's lover didn't kill him because Orton had put him in a play.

HENRY. I didn't mean –

SAM. He killed him because he was jealous of the success. At least that's certainly the point Lahr was making –

HENRY. I just meant – You know. He was trying to *threaten*.

Beat.

Keith was. So he chose –

Beat.

But of course he was only joking. It was like a literary joke.

Beat.

You know Keith.

SAM. I have to say, not that well, it's usually Mary . . . at parties . . .

HENRY. A lot smarter than you'd at first think.

Beat.

Reading all the time, Sam. Of course not exactly the type of stuff you or I, you know. But reading. (*Laughs.*) Someday I am going to target him as my audience. I'd like to try that. To write for people like him. It'd be interesting to try to write a book that could be published in the *Daily Mail*. (*Laughs.*) My books obviously to him were bullshit.

Short pause.

A good boy though. He wouldn't have hurt me for . . .

SAM. Of course not.

Short pause.

HENRY. What beautiful hair on that boy.

Beat.

SAM. Sorry!

HENRY. Really, let me move the wheelchair to –

SAM. I keep bumping.

HENRY. It's no trouble.

Pause.

SAM (*finally*). You know Jack and Beth.

HENRY. What about them? They aren't – ?

SAM. No, no.

Beat.

They're fine.

Beat.

It's just that they won't talk to me either. This is according to Mary, of course. They talk to her.

Beat.

Daily. Maybe hourly.

Beat.

To – as she puts it – 'commiserate'.

HENRY. Are they in your book too?

SAM. I wouldn't say that.

Beat.

Certainly in no way that could ever give offence. I do not use names. I do not use their looks. Just because we took them to our place on Cape Cod –

HENRY. I didn't know you and Jack and Beth were –

SAM. We aren't.

Beat.

We aren't close at all. We offered and . . . you know. Somehow they accepted. Anyway –

HENRY. I hear Cape Cod is beautiful.

SAM. You should –

Beat.

When you have the time. If you're going to be in the States anyway –

HENRY. Let's talk about that later. We have all afternoon, don't we?

SAM. Yeah.

Beat.

Goddamn right we do. (*Laughs.*) So – Cape Cod. Jack and Beth loved it. They weren't much trouble either.

Beat.

I thought they would be, especially Jack, but I was pleasantly surprised.

HENRY. Good for Jack.

SAM. So – there's this bit, this very small bit in the novel about this English woman who is visiting Cape Cod and there are one or two things that happen to her – that the narrator actually fantasises as

happening to her. This is what people are not getting that there is
fantasy in this book.

HENRY (*as if quoting*). A work of the imagination.

SAM. Yeah. Yeah. And so the character has sex with a teenage boy on
the beach one night. I made this up. I swear I did. I am not saying
Beth had sex with a teenager on the beach.

Beat.

Where do I ever say that?!

Beat.

And if she did, Henry, well – I certainly am not supposed to know
about it.

Short pause.

HENRY. And Jack?

SAM. I am told by reliable sources that he would like to hurt me.

Beat.

But I am also told, Henry, that this has done a lot for their marriage.
But do I get credit for that?! No way!

Beat.

Hell, as a couple they were pretty boring. I didn't even give the
character a husband. I had no use for their relationship at all.

HENRY. Jack writes. He should understand.

SAM. Essays. That makes it worse. He thinks if you use anything there
should be footnotes.

HENRY. Maybe in this case you should suggest – (*Laughs.*)

SAM (*laughs*). Good idea! Serve them right! The literalmindedness.
You'd think I was writing his wife's goddamn biography.

Beat.

Anyway Mary thinks they might sue.

HENRY. How cheap.

Beat.

What does Anton say?

SAM. I'm waiting to see if Jack has the guts. If he does then I'll tell
Anton who will then get sick.

Beat.

I know my editor.

Short pause.

Sometimes you have to ask yourself – where is the support? Where are the people who are supposed to be on your side?

Beat.

You were saying, Henry, you gave Keith the galleys for *The Lefthand.*

HENRY. *Hand*er.

SAM. I did the same thing with Mary. This is when it started.

Beat.

Now this is my wife. This is the person who is supposed to help me.

Beat.

As she's reading, she keeps looking up at me, biting her lower lip, twitching her neck like she was cold.

Beat.

And oh was she ever cold, Henry!

Beat.

Had I only known.

Beat.

I watch her close the galleys, and then I say rather cutely – 'well?' Big question mark, big question mark. You know how you feel, you're nervous. You're frightened. You try to make a joke – 'Pretty bad, huh?' And then she says, and I quote, Henry: 'I hope the warehouse where the books are kept burns to the ground. I hope all typed copies somehow mysteriously disappear – if there is a God they will – and finally I pray with all my might that all ten of your fingers atrophy and drop off, hopefully with terrible pain, assuming, that is, that you can still feel pain or any other human emotion – and then this atrocity will go on no longer.'

Pause.

HENRY. I want to read this book.

SAM. It's very funny. Philip Roth wrote me a personal note, he loved it.

HENRY. Well then, he's a writer.

SAM. That's right.

Beat.

That is right.

Beat.

So, I laughed when Mary says this. 'Atrocity, Mary?' I say 'aren't we a wee bit exaggerating? I mean, the Holocaust was an atrocity.' But she goes into the kitchen and I hear her rummaging around in the cabinets. My first thought was that she's going to get a knife.

HENRY. Mary would never . . .

SAM. What can I say? So I have a vivid imagination. And I'm thinking – knife. And then I start to think that Anton, my erstwhile editor, will have a field day with my murder. You English may not have any guts but when there's a murder you are great; right in there, routing around.

Beat.

But she doesn't come out with a knife. She comes out with a package of letters. The letters I had written her when she was still in school.

HENRY. She keeps them in the kitchen?

SAM. That tells you something.

HENRY. Fascinating.

SAM. Isn't it.

HENRY. There's a story there.

SAM. I'm writing it. I was working on it this morning.

HENRY. Good.

SAM. And she throws them in my face.

Short pause.

After she left I started to read them. They're pretty well written.

HENRY. When did Mary actually walk out then?

SAM. It took her forever, Henry. It took weeks. (*Laughs to himself.*) Just like the wife in my novel.

HENRY. Do you know where she is?

SAM. Her sister came – Jean, not Helen who's the one you know. She's the nice one who danced that time with Keith.

HENRY. Helen, I remember her.

SAM. She's back in Boston.

HENRY. Ah.

SAM. Jean's here for something or other.

HENRY. I see.

SAM. So Jean got some of Mary's things this morning. I asked her rather politely where my wife was – and you'd have thought I'd tried to rape her.

Beat.

I didn't put Jean in the book. In the next one I won't make that mistake again.

Pause and the scene begins to fade out.

Anyway, I thought I'd go by the play she's in one night –

HENRY (*a bit drunk now*). She's not in the Tom Howard?!

SAM. No, no.

Beat.

Her? She'd never take a job that pays.

Fade out.

Scene 3
HENRY'S TALE OF COURAGE.

The restaurant. A while later.

SAM. Sixty thousand dollars? Jesus. And you have to teach what? Twice a week? Three times a week?

HENRY. There'll be two seminars. I could do them both in one day, I suppose.

SAM. One day a week for sixty thousand dollars. Where'd you hear about this job? How come I never hear about these jobs?

HENRY. They called me. Through a friend of a friend.

Beat.

I guess at some party or whatever sometime I said – in the abstract – that I'd like to spend time in the States. That I like to teach. And two plus two and so forth.

Beat.

I guess.

Beat.

No one's actually told me how my name –

WAITER. Excuse me. Would you like coffee? Dessert?

HENRY. Coffee for me I think.

SAM. The same.

HENRY. And what about a whiskey? Two Jamesons?

SAM. I've got nothing to do today.

WAITER. Two Jamesons.

Waiter goes.

SAM. What does your doctor say? The winters are very cold in Upstate New York.

HENRY. My doctor says I can do anything I want. Go anywhere I want.

Beat.

Drink anything I want.

SAM. You've got to give me the name of this doctor. (*Laughs.*) What does Keith say? He must be very excited.

HENRY. Sure.

Beat.

Yes.

Long pause.

SAM. What about housing? Do they have a place –

HENRY. I figure I shall just rent a flat. It couldn't be –

SAM. No, no, get them to give you some housing help. They expect that. So negotiate for it.

Beat.

They expect it but it is up to you to ask.

Beat.

They own houses. You could get a whole house.

Beat.

It's worth asking about, Henry.

Pause.

HENRY. New scenery. The change. (*Suddenly energised.*) To me it is all about pushing all the crap away for a while and getting back to what really matters, Sam!!

Beat.

There is so much crap. One only wants to get on with it.

Beat.

So one tries to find a new space; some place with life in it. What she has done to this country, Sam.

SAM. The States are no –

HENRY. There, I wouldn't care. I wouldn't have to.

Beat.

You understand that.

Beat.

I think that in some place different I could be alone. In a way, I guess that's what I'm looking for. Ever since I was in school I thought that that was what being a writer was all about. That that was the attraction, Sam. That was what being an artist means.

SAM. To be by yourself?

HENRY. To follow your own thoughts – you know – and dreams. To discover!

Beat.

And leave other people to do the other things.

SAM. This is attractive. Sure.

Pause.

HENRY. You know last summer Keith and I got a cottage on Jura. The Hebrides.

Beat.

Pretty much the same place as George Orwell had when he was writing *Nineteen Eighty-Four.*

SAM. You're not sure?

HENRY. It might have been.

Beat.

It probably was.

Beat.

The nights were as peaceful as anything I've ever experienced. And the people . . . Call me strange but I like the Scots. I really don't think they're so gloomy.

Beat.

My agent, George Hopewell –

SAM. I know George.

HENRY. He came up for a few days and went fishing.

Short pause.

SAM. The whole thing sounds ideal, Henry.

HENRY. To me.

Beat.

To you.

Beat.

Being isolated from the world does not frighten us.

Beat.

We live for it, in a way, don't we?

Beat.

Keith left after four days. He said he had started to listen to the blood flow through his head. I told him to see a doctor. One or two crazy things he did –

Beat.

You don't want to know.

Beat.

So – Keith left. Or for a while I thought he'd drowned. He had said nothing to me. I was a wreck of course. I got no work done. Not a lick, Sam.

Beat.

Oh well.

Beat.

He came back to London is what he did. I'd forgotten I'd given him a set of keys to the flat. So he was happy. He had a friend visit with him while I was gone.

Pause.

SAM. So at least he was safe.

HENRY (*laughs to himself*). I suppose so.

Short pause.

So George came up to hold my hand and he went fishing while I pretended to write.

Beat.

WAITER. Two Jamesons?

HENRY. Thank you.

SAM. Thanks.

Pause as they sip.

HENRY. A brilliant fly fisherman, George. When he retires that's what he's going to do.

SAM. How old is he now anyway?

HENRY. George?

Beat.

I don't know. Seventy? Who knows.

Short pause.

But anyway the whole summer wasn't a complete loss. I did start to read Orwell again. What an extraordinary man. I've already planned him as the first subject of my public lectures at Cornell.

SAM. You have to give – ?

HENRY. Two. One in the Fall. One in the Spring. To show me off. For sixty thousand dollars they need something to show off.

Beat.

But I can choose.

Short pause.

What I'd like to concentrate on is the man's courage. He gives us all strength today. Or he should at least. He certainly does me.

Beat.

You know of course he was dying when he wrote *Nineteen Eighty-Four*. He knew it too. He tried to hide it.

Beat.

He could even joke about it. And he certainly denied it when he was asked.

Beat.

When someone was crude enough to ask.

Beat.

Or cared enough to ask.

Beat.

In fact I have a thesis that I plan to propose that the wisdom of this great book derives in part from the fact that he was dying.

Beat.

You feel that somehow.

Beat.

A dying man's last cry. But a cry that is not about himself, but about his world. That is where the real courage is. That is the heroism.

Beat.

At such a point to think about the world.

Beat.

To care about what happens.

Pause.

I should tell you, Sam – Keith, he died last week.

SAM. Henry, I – !

HENRY *I* just found out myself yesterday.

SAM. Oh shit. Henry –

HENRY. His mother flew in from Jamaica to take care of him.

Beat.

She wouldn't let me see him.

Beat.

Or near him.

Beat.

We talked once on the phone about four weeks ago.

Short pause.

The Irish know how to make whiskey, don't they.

SAM. Henry, I'm sorry. Mary didn't –

HENRY. She doesn't know. As I said, I found out just last night. And I guess it still hasn't sunk in. He was a beautiful man, Sam.

Beat.

A gentle man.

Beat.

I loved him very very much.

Pause.

So – (*Sighs.*) I haven't of course been officially offered the Cornell job. There have only been letters . . .

Beat.

I meet next month with a gentleman from the school. Though I expect . . .

SAM *Pro forma.*

HENRY. Why shouldn't it be?

Beat.

Though no one there has actually seen me.

Beat.

Perhaps I'll be out of the wheelchair by then.

Pause.

SAM. Do you know if there was a funeral?

HENRY. I don't know, Sam.

Short pause.

SAM. Who called you?

HENRY. I think it was his brother.

Beat.

I think. He didn't say.

Pause.

(*With sudden energy.*) Orwell I think needed this knowledge of his dying to make his book.

Beat.

It gave him the clarity. Do you understand?!

SAM. I think –

HENRY. And so in this sense – in dying he gave us the gift of his vision. Sam, he died to help us all see. To help us know. To help us stop what he could see in his death was happening to the world!

Beat.

(*Very passionate now.*) Art can do that!

Beat.

Words can!

Pause, then fade out.

Scene 4
THE SEARCH FOR A NEW INN.

A short while later. SAM *pushes* HENRY *in his wheelchair through the noisy crowded streets of the West End. This, quite a change from the soft whispers of the restaurant.* HENRY *and* SAM *are fairly drunk by now.*

HENRY. I think it's up here.

SAM (*to a passerby*). Excuse me. Excuse . . . Sorry.

HENRY. Off a little street.

Beat.

It's the only decent pub around here. There's a room in the back that's usually fairly quiet.

SAM. No darts?

Beat.

Please, I do not like sitting in a room and dodging darts while I drink. Why this is such a British tradition –

HENRY. Here! Turn here!

SAM (*to a passerby*). Excuse us. Please. Watch it.

Beat.

Move please.

Beat.

We're trying –

Beat.

Could you – ? Get out of the way for chrissake! The man's in a wheelchair!!

Obviously the crowd has moved.

SAM. Thank you. Thank you! You're very kind all of you!

Short pause as they continue.

HENRY. You should have pushed Rocinante right at them. That's what my sister does.

SAM. Rocinante? It has a name?

Beat.

Henry, you named your wheelchair Rocinante?

HENRY. Is something wrong with that?

SAM. No, no. (*Laughs.*)

HENRY. Why is that funny?

SAM. It's just – Then for this afternoon at least, then that should make me –

HENRY. You are much too skinny for my idea of Sancho Panza, Sam.

Beat.

Much.

Beat.

But if that is who you wish to be, I shall not stand in your way. This decision I leave up to you. There! That's the pub there!! (*To passerby.*) Get out of the way!!!

Fade out.

Scene 5
THE KNIGHT ERRANT AND SANCHO ENCOUNTER AN UGLY VISION.

The back room of a very crowded and noisy pub. HENRY is at a table, waiting for SAM to get drinks from the bar. A YOUNG WOMAN sits very close to HENRY, crowded in at the next table.

YOUNG WOMAN. Excuse me, is someone using that ashtray?

HENRY. What? No. We don't – I used to, but –

Beat.

Please. Take it. It's yours.

Beat.

Here.

Beat.

Smoke doesn't bother me. Really.

SAM (*approaching the table*). Sorry. I thought people worked in the afternoon. Could you move in please.

Beat.

I'm not that skinny. Thank you.

Beat.

(*To Henry.*) Jesus. No Jameson, but they had Bushmills.

HENRY. Oh that's fine. Bushmills is fine, Sam.

They are both quite a bit drunk by now.

SAM. Anyway –

He sits.

Cheers.

HENRY. Cheers.

SAM. You feel okay?

HENRY. This'll help. (*Drinks.*)

SAM. I feel great. I really feel great.

HENRY. I thought it'd be quieter!

SAM. It's fine. Really. It's great.

HENRY. This young woman here borrowed our ashtray.

YOUNG WOMAN. What? You want it back?

SAM. No, no.

Beat.

No. Of course. Our compliments. (*Laughs.*) They really do pack them in here. Anyway –

Short pause.

Henry, I was thinking how funny it was going to be; me in England, you in America.

Beat.

Me in *your* country, *you* in –

HENRY. I understand what you were saying.

SAM. It's like they've chased us both away.

HENRY. You're right. That is exactly what they've done. And don't for a minute kid yourself, *that* has been their goal all along. If they get rid of people like us . . . us . . .

SAM. I know. I know.

HENRY. You take the artist out of his society, either by force or –

Beat.

The way they've done it to us, Sam. They way they've done it to you and the way they are doing it to me. Then who is left to stop them? Who is left to stand up and say '*J'accuse! J'accuse!*'

Beat.

You see what I am saying.

SAM. Uh-huh. What you say, it . . . for me . . . You are touching something . . .

Beat.

I've been away from home for eleven long years, Henry. I took my wife. I took my kids.

Beat.

My wife came home; she's English, but my kids. But me? You know I wonder – You see what happened and I wonder – And you too at Cornell, you too will wonder, Henry, watching the news, following what is happening in your own country from afar; from – a great distance, Henry. And you wonder – At least I do.

Beat.

What if I had stayed in America? Could I have helped? Could I have changed things? It is a mess there, Henry.

HENRY. Ugly!

SAM. An ugly mess. And it will get worse before it gets better.

HENRY. That is always the way.

SAM (*suddenly energised*). What could I have done? What could I have written that – ? What? What?

Beat.

Hmmmmm.

Pause. Pub noise.

HENRY *I* think – and I am not even sure I believe this myself, but for the sake of argument, Sam – *I* think the artist today – in today's world – is given *too* much responsibility.

SAM. I do not agree at all! Henry, if anything –

HENRY. Let me finish!

Beat.

We should be working for the future, Sam, writing about what is *immortal*, for Christ's sake, about what *doesn't* change.

SAM. I'm agreeing with something you said a little while ago. What was that you said?

HENRY. When did I say this?

SAM. A short time ago.

Short pause.

Anyway, I agree. At first I disagreed and now I agree.

Short pause.

I feel I was a coward to leave my country.

HENRY. You are being very hard –

SAM. A coward.

HENRY. If you think that, then go –

SAM. Mary hates New York.

Beat.

The only auditions she gets is for Shaw plays. She hates Shaw plays.

HENRY. I thought Mary left you.

SAM. She'll come back. She's angry that's all. She'll forget about the book. It is only a book.

Short pause.

They are scared of us, Henry!!

He has shouted this. Pub noise quiets for a moment as people turn towards SAM; then noise picks up again.

(*Continuing*). That's how you know that you matter, because they're scared of you.

Beat.

They put us in jail, don't they? All over the world they do this.

HENRY. You've never been put into jail. What do you write that could get you thrown into jail?

Beat.

Me too! I'm not just saying you!

Short pause.

What do I write about? I write about a world that is cold to people like me.

SAM. My world is cold and unfeeling and –

HENRY. So we write the obvious. So you think we should be shot for that?

Beat.

That we could be shot for that?!

Beat.

I write love stories.

SAM. Gay love stories. Now in England today –

HENRY. Don't tell me about England today!!!

Pause. Pub noise.

SAM. So – you are running away.

HENRY. I am not running away. I am getting away.

Short pause.

SAM. Why do we hate our countries? Why do we abandon our homes?

Beat.

Hmmmm. Makes you sad when you put it that way.

Short pause.

If I had only stayed, think about what I could have done.

HENRY. Stop saying that.

SAM. I could have changed things, Henry.

HENRY. You couldn't have done shit? Who does shit?

SAM. Alexander Solzhenitzyn, he did shit, Henry.

HENRY. You are not Solzhen –

SAM. I'm saying – do we have a choice anymore?!!

Beat.

(*Louder.*) Do you?!!!

Beat.

Being gay! In your case, being gay. In England. In my case, believing in a society that takes responsibility for itself, for its people, which helps –

HENRY. Sam –

YOUNG WOMAN. Excuse me. But I couldn't help overhearing.

SAM. What – ?

YOUNG WOMAN. You're both some sort of writer, I take it.

SAM. What do you want?

YOUNG WOMAN. What do you write – mysteries? Novels?

SAM. Novels.

Beat.

YOUNG WOMAN. Well, I know it's none of my business, but your whole conversation seems to me to be, well . . . It's bull, isn't it?

SAM. Who asked –

YOUNG WOMAN. I mean, you keep talking about how a writer matters – or maybe it's what he writes that matters. I don't think you have the distinction very clear in your minds, by the way. But that is a minor point.

Beat.

So how do you matter? Would you like an objective opinion?

SAM. Henry, who is this woman?

YOUNG WOMAN. First, let me remind you that this is 1989, gentleman. And this is the real world.

Pub has been listening and suddenly cheers with this last line.

Try to keep your applause until the end please.

Beat.

So, *you* are an American, I gather.

SAM. That's right.

YOUNG WOMAN. Then I would have thought that *you'd* at least know better. But I take it you've been away for some time so that will explain it.

SAM. Explain what?

YOUNG WOMAN. I was in San Diego once, just last year for a sales conference and let me tell you I had the time of my life. The weather – I could just live there forever! But it wasn't just sunshine and sand that got me – there was a spirit in the air. Call it whatever: and energy, American confidence, whatever, but it was there and it was beautiful, let me tell you.

Beat.

What Ronald Reagan has accomplished . . . the world should be on its knees in thanks and I do not exaggerate. That man is a hero.

Beat.

There is a sense of freedom in your country that you feel in an instant. An entrepreneurial freedom that has given hope to all of us really. After all it is what we are trying to achieve in England now.

Beat.

In part of England now.

Beat.

It is a very exciting time, isn't it?

Beat.

But I digress. Getting back to you two. To you two writers. To you two 'intellectuals'.

SAM. I didn't say we were –

YOUNG WOMAN. Bull. Any more bullshit from you and we'll all start floating out of here. If I called you an intellectual, you'd be flattered, right?

SAM. Sure. Of course, I –

YOUNG WOMAN. So obviously what you are not aware of is that this word has come to be used today only pejoratively. Am I right?

Crowd in pub yells agreement.

It's come to mean what? Bullshitter, right? The sort of guys who sit on their asses and talk all day as if talking ever mattered for shit, ever changed anything.

SAM. Look, I don't agree.

YOUNG WOMAN. Oh, now he wants to argue!

She laughs, others laugh.

Look, I'm in the real world, OK? You want to know what that is? Listen to what I did today.

Beat.

I'm trying to sell this Japanese guy this boat. This is lunch. For him it's going to cost about what an okay breakfast costs in Tokyo. I'm talking about the boat not the lunch. (*She laughs.*) He's just been transferred here and he's got to buy something, and I've got this boat or my company does.

Beat.

Full kitchen, microwave, colour TV. A big goddamn boat. This is my assignment. Why? Because I speak Japanese? Are you kidding? It's because I've got the biggest breasts in the company. And rumour has it – which by the way I now think is true – so, the word is that these Japanese like 'em big breasted, sort of novelty for them I guess.

Beat.

In the office, we had a whole meeting over whether I'd wear a bra or not. This company is thorough.

Beat.

So today we have lunch. The boat he buys before we've even ordered. By coffee, he's in such a good mood he takes the whole company and I'm made Vice President.

Beat.

I think it's Vice President. The interpreter had his mouth full when he told me. Maybe it's President. I don't know.

Beat.

Some main course, huh? (*She laughs.*) And there you have the real world.

Some applause from the crowd.

Now don't get me wrong; I think I deserve this promotion, whatever it is. I worked hard for it. I arrived on time at the restaurant. I laughed at two very confusing jokes translated from the Japanese.

Beat.

I laughed before one was even translated.

Beat.

No. I earned this. I certainly did. And just as soon as my former bosses are given the old heave-ho, as they say in San Diego, I'm going back there and claiming my rightful office, be it the President's or the Vice President's. But if it is the latter, then you can all bet your bottom dollar – or pound – on what position I'll be gunning for next week.

Some applause, then people are coming up to her and offering her congratulations, a job well done, nice work, etc. fade out.

Scene 6
THE ENCOUNTER IN THE INN IS LEFT FAR BEHIND.

(*St James Park. Late afternoon. SAM pushes HENRY in the wheelchair. Birdsong, some traffic noise in the distance, but the sense of quiet and peace after the pub.*)

SAM. Did that really happen?

HENRY. What?

SAM. In the pub. That woman. Those people applauding and congratulating her.

HENRY. I couldn't hear. It was too noisy.

SAM. Oh.

Beat.

You didn't hear?

HENRY. I'm drunk, what about you?

SAM. Is there any other way to be?

Short pause.

HENRY. Anyway, they say that satellite photos show a quarter or something of the whole Amazon jungle is on fire.

Beat.

Or been burned up already.

Beat.

Not quite a quarter. That can't be.

SAM. Whatever.

HENRY. The destruction, it's – imagine.

Beat.

You can't picture it. It's like some global deathwish is upon us, Sam. Things are bad. Wherever you look.

Short pause.

So the idea for the story is about some peasants. I haven't thought this through. I haven't let myself. I know I'll never write it.

Beat.

Peasants, and I do a kind of thing Golding has done. Even if it does sound pretentious.

SAM. So you risk it. We risk pretentiousness every day.

HENRY. The peasants, they're not from the jungle. They have escaped to there; refugees say from a revolution.

SAM. Very *Lord of the Flies.*

HENRY. To a point.

Beat.

Maybe. I don't know. Yes, but different.

Beat.

So we start by liking these people. They're peasants; poor, they've run from the fascists. They're here to build a new life for themselves in the Amazon jungle.

SAM. The revolution was a right-wing revolution?

HENRY. That's right.

SAM (*stopping the wheelchair*). Henry. Over there.

HENRY. The man or the woman?

SAM. The swans, Henry.

HENRY. I never understood the attraction in feeding swans. *You* stand in *their* shit, throwing *them* food *you'd* otherwise throw out. The poetic justice of this I get, but where is the joy?

SAM. I'll keep pushing. Giddy-up Rocinante.

HENRY. If you want a rest – Let's find a bench. We've passed a million empty benches. For some reason St James Park doesn't have the drawing power of the pubs we've been in.

SAM. I'd rather keep walking.

HENRY. If you wish.

Beat.

Lead on, I am in your hands, Sancho.

Short pause.

Of course I've never been to the Amazon. Or any jungle for that matter. So for details I figure I'd end up a little stuck.

SAM. There are books.

HENRY. Still. One wouldn't have the *experience* . . . I mean Kew Gardens is not really very close, is it?

Beat.

Anyway, as we are talking about books we shall *never* write –

Beat.

My peasants settle in the jungle. But what do they know about jungles? Nothing, Sam. So the first thing they do is try to change it. They begin to clear the land. Literally start burning down everything. This is the only way they know how to survive.

SAM. By destroying?

HENRY. That's what it looks like. They are actually trying to create fields, but from the distance of a satellite, it looks like wanton destruction.

Short pause.

Now a team of Western conservationists – good people – journey into this jungle.

Beat.

They tell the peasants that without the vegetation of jungles like these – and there aren't many left for Christ's sake – the world needs the oxygen the jungles give off. They create the necessary atmosphere for human life.

Beat.

The peasants listen but they are thinking: what about us? How do *we* eat?

Beat.

The conservationists promise a massive amount of help – both food and technical advice.

Beat.

At last the peasants give in and stop the burning. The world is saved. At least from this and at least for now.

Beat.

As for the peasants, the food and help never reaches them; the government won't allow it; and now without the fires, the government soldiers venture into the jungle and either kill or arrest all the peasants.

Beat.

And that's the end.

Beat.

Of course I'll never write it.

SAM. Because you've never been to a jungle?

HENRY *Because* – it is too goddamn despairing.

Short pause.

Total despair may indeed be what I'm feeling.

Beat.

For us. For our countries.

Beat.

Certainly for my country.

Beat.

But it isn't what I want to be expressing, what I need to express.

Beat.

And that's hope, Sam. Even if it's but some modicum of hope, still that's what we need to be saying, isn't it?

Beat.

That is what is needed.

Beat.

When you know that you're dying, you don't want to be told that you're dead.

Long pause. As they pass by the pond, swans cry out.

So what's your – ?

SAM. I don't have –

HENRY. Come on. Come on.

Short pause.

SAM. I've got one that is also set in the jungle.

A bird cries out.

HENRY. Bullshit. Come on.

SAM. I'm serious. I do. I even started to write it once.

HENRY. If you're pulling my –

SAM. I'm not!!

Short pause.

The main character's a painter. American. And what he paints is flowers and fauna of the jungle.

Beat.

I'm getting thirsty, aren't you?

HENRY. Go toward the river. I think I know an off-licence.

Short pause.

SAM. This painter, he spends months alone in the jungle painting his pictures. He's one of those artists who have removed themselves from the world.

Beat.

Or rather that is what I want the reader to first think, that the bloke is rather in another world. Nice guy, sure, but – not like you or me.

Beat.

But then we start to see that his pictures, besides being beautiful in their own right – and I am not underestimating this – besides their beauty, we see what they actually accomplish: with these pictures he has discovered flowers that the world hasn't even known existed, including one that blooms only once and this only in the middle of the night, in a jungle full of snakes and poisonous spiders. He has seen such a flower and he has painted it.

Beat.

Painted it for the whole world, you could say.

Beat.

So this painter then is also a discoverer, isn't he?

Short pause.

And on the other hand, as you have said about the jungle, so much is being destroyed now, this painter then is also recording for the future what we have already killed.

Beat.

He is preserving life. He is reminding us what we once had.

Beat.

He is a conscience then. In a way, he is.

Pause.

Just by painting flowers. (*Laughs to himself.*) Of course, he'd never say that about himself. He'd say, he paints what's in front of him, what strikes *him* as interesting or beautiful or fascinating. And that most of his time is involved in the minutiae of that work: choosing colours, learning about new paints, canvases that don't wrinkle in the jungle humidity.

Short pause.

And if you were to get him talking about how *he* sees what he does, you'd end up hearing about what he thinks of other painters, about getting money for his journeys, about the difficulties of travel, what he likes to eat, the flies, the snakes, where to buy boots.

Pause.

That's it. That's as far as I've ever gotten with this story.

Pause.

But I've never been to a jungle either. So I better stick to what I know . . .

Short pause.

HENRY. Like marriage.

SAM. Why not?

HENRY. Or trips to Cape Cod with English friends.

Beat.

Wives and lost love letters.

SAM. The difficulties of living in another's country.

Beat.

HENRY. Tom Howard's plays.

Beat.

SAM. Where to buy comfortable walking shoes.

HENRY. You haven't even mentioned walking shoes.

SAM. I didn't think you'd be interested, Henry.

As they stroll: fade out.

Scene 7
UPON A BRIDGE COMFORT IS FOUND.

Westminster Bridge. The sound of buses and cars going by is heard throughout, sometimes even drowning out what is being said; also boat horns in the distance and once or twice a train.

Pause. HENRY is alone in his wheelchair. SAM hurries from a distance.

SAM (*calls*). There you are! (*He runs.*) How'd you get this far out?

HENRY. I wheeled myself. We can do that, you know.

SAM. When you weren't by the steps, I thought you'd –

HENRY. Did you find the off-licence?

Beat.

SAM. Yeah. Here. We're back to Jameson.

HENRY. I won't complain.

Pause. They drink out of the bottle.

SAM. Quite the view.

HENRY (*begins to recite Matthew Arnold's 'Dover Beach', making a few small mistakes.*)
'The sea is calm to-night.
The tide is full, the moon lies fair
Upon the Straits; – on the French coast, the light
Gleams, and is gone; the cliffs of England stand,
Glimmering and vast, out in the tranquil bay.
Come to a window, sweet is the night air!
Only, from the long line of spray
Where the ebb meets the moon-blanch'd sand,
Listen! you hear a grating roar
Of pebbles which the waves suck back, and fling,
At their return, up the high strand,
Begin, and cease, and then again begin,
With tremulous cadence slow, and bring
The eternal sadness in.

Ah, love, let us be true
To one another! for the world, which seems
To lie before us like a land of dreams,
So various, so beautiful, so new,
Hath really neither joy, nor love, nor light,
Nor certitude, nor peace, nor help for pain;
And we are here as on a darkling plain
Swept with confused alarms of struggle and flight,
Where ignorant armies clash by night.'

That's pretty close, but don't quote me. (*Laughs.*) But not bad after thirty-five years. Amazing what stays in your head.

SAM. What grows in your head.

Beat.

HENRY. What you find in your head and begin to understand.

Short pause. Bus goes by.

It's not Dover Beach, but the Thames will do.

Short pause.

SAM. Now how about 'Westminster Bridge', since that's rather appropriate, considering where we are standing.

HENRY. Sorry. Never had to learn it.

Beat.

Don't know it.

Takes bottle and drinks.

Cheers.

Short pause.

Are we drunk yet?

SAM. I think we must be.

HENRY. Good.

Pause. Then SAM *hands* HENRY *a bag.*

SAM. Here.

HENRY (*opening the bag*). Is this what you've been carrying. I thought it looked like a book.

SAM. I bought it for you, Henry. That's why I was late.

Beat.

It was in a window . . .

Beat.

I had no trouble getting a tube, I just stopped when I saw . . .

Short pause.

HENRY. This I doubt. Not about stopping, but that you bought this for me.

SAM. Henry –

HENRY. That doesn't mean I won't take it, Sam.

Beat.

I'm taking it.

Short pause.

Thank you.

He has opened the book; it is an early edition of Walt Whitman's
Leaves of Grass. *He has opened to 'A song of joys'.*

'O to make the most jubilant song!
Full of music – full of manhood, womanhood,
infancy!'

Beat.

I wonder if Clause 28 can ban public readings of Walt Whitman.

Short pause.

Here. You read some. It's better in an American accent.

SAM *takes the book.*

SAM. It's an early printing of the 1892 deathbed edition.

HENRY. I know, I know.

Short pause.

SAM *begins to read sections of 'A song of joys'; as he does, buses,
cars, people pass them on the bridge, often drowning out what is
being read.*

SAM (*reading*).
  'O for the voices of animals – O for the swiftness and balance of
    fishes!
  O for the dropping of raindrops in a song!
  O for the sunshine and motion of waves in a song!

  O the joy of my spirit – it is uncaged it darts like lightning!
  It is not enough to have this globe or a certain time,
  I will have thousands of globes and all time.

*The harbour, bridge are alive with sound – buses, cars, people, trains,
Big Ben, etc.*

  'O to go back to the place where I was born,
  To hear the birds sing once more,
  To ramble about the house and barn and over the fields once
    more,
  And through the orchard and along the old lanes once more.'

SAM *turns a page and finds another section.*

'O to sail to sea in a ship!
To leave this steady unendurable land,
To leave the tiresome sameness of the streets, the sidewalks and the
  houses,
To leave you O you solid motionless land, and entering a ship,
To sail and sail and sail!'

Pause. Harbour and birdge noise. SAM *hands* HENRY *back the book.*

Here.

HENRY. Thank you. I will cherish it for as long as I live.

Short pause.

What do you want to do now?

SAM. I don't know.

Beat.

There are some book stalls on the South Bank.

HENRY. The ones by the National Theatre?

SAM. Yeah. They're not much –

HENRY. They're not that bad. What the hell. What's the harm in having a look, I always say.

Beat.

Unless you have to –

SAM. No.

Beat.

I have nowhere I want to go.

HENRY. Good.

They begin to go across the bridge.

You want a drink?

SAM. Sure. Thanks. (*He drinks.*)

Train goes by.

(*As they go; to passerby.*) Excuse us. Sorry.

Beat.

Watch it. Sorry.

Beat.

Could you move please. Thank you.

Pause.

HENRY. You know, when I die, it's not people I'll miss, it's their words.

Pause, they go, leaving only traffic noise behind them, which finally fades out.

BY WHERE THE OLD SHED USED TO BE

a play for radio by Craig Warner

For Shannon McCarthy

Craig Warner was born in Hollywood in 1964. He moved to New York City in 1985 and the following year directed a production of his stage play *Matthias* at Cooper Square Theatre. In 1987 he moved to London, and shortly thereafter his play *God's Country* was produced by the Angel Playwright Scheme and Dina and Alexander E. Racolin at the Old Red Lion Theatre Club in Islington, directed by Richard Hansom. His work for BBC radio includes Caroline Raphael's production of *Great Men of Music* as part of the first annual Young Playwrights Festival (the play was also translated and produced in West Germany for WDR); Andy Jordan's production of *Love to Madeleine*, and a translation of Maupassant's 'The Baptism' into English. The author would like to acknowledge his debts to Micheline Steinberg, Penny Gold, Lloyd Trott, Cíara Heenan, and of course the very talented Andy Jordan.

By Where the Old Shed Used to Be was first broadcast on BBC Radio 3,
'Drama Now' on 12 December 1989. The cast was as follows:

CREATOR (A woman in her fifties)	Mary Wimbush
AGEING PUBLIC SCHOOLBOY	Simon Treves
OLD MAN	Hubert Tucker
FISHWIFE	Wendy Brierley
DEBORAH (Getting on for fifty)	June Barrie
POLICE CONSTABLE	David Goudge
SERGEANT	Eric Allen
SARAH	Siobhan Redmond
LOUISE (The Younger)	Tilly Vosburgh
ADELAIDE (The Elder)	Miranda Richardson
FACTORY WORKER	Simon Treves
WILLIAM	Anton Lesser
FRANK	Peter-Hugo Daly
CLAIRE	Judy Parfitt
POLICE CHIEF	Christopher Ettridge
BARMAN	Anthony Donovan
FIREMAN	Anthony Donovan
MINISTER	David King
GUARD	David Goudge
FARMER (Same voice as OLD MAN)	Hubert Tucker

Director: Andy Jordan
Running time, as broadcast: approximately 100 minutes

Music was composed by Simon Jeffes and performed by members of the Penguin Café Orchestra.

CREATOR. Turn down the lights. It's late in the evening, late in the year, and where we're going the life is all in the dark. The ones with no homes have scattered like beetles to the doorways and between buildings, and all the good women have gone home. And there is wind. Wind, please.

Wind.

Wind. Now there are three parts to every city, and three kinds of wind. There's the place where they go to work, and at night the wind ruffles no hair, sends no ties whipping, only locks this morning's news waving on the leg of a bench. There's the place where they live, where the wind is bedsheets and a choir of teakettles. And there's the place we've come to now. Wind: the flapping of skirts. The clicking of heels. The slick, sharp swish of rattails slipping between the stones. Tables overturned, blades out: the fanning of lashes. They call this place the harbour, but the few boats that remain are shells, disused; corseted in barnacles, they lull dreamily and rock like drowned girls.

AGEING PUBLIC SCHOOLBOY. An appropriate assimile . . .

CREATOR. Is it?

AGEING PUBLIC SCHOOLBOY. . . . for not three months have gone by since a sixteen-year-old girl was found badly decomposed under a yacht.

OLD MAN. How did they identify her?

AGEING PUBLIC SCHOOLBOY. Her makeup floated to the top and formed a perfect impression of her face looking up in a ripple. The police pressed the ripple with blotting paper, peeled it back, and once it was dry they made copies for general distribution.

OLD MAN. A feat of modern intelligence!

FISHWIFE. It was a feat she made it to sixteen! If all the men who been through her joined hands the two on either end could kiss in China!

CREATOR. If you could please just wait till I introduced you . . .

FISHWIFE. You're not going to introduce us because we're not in this play.

AGEING PUBLIC SCHOOLBOY. They haven't given us a play today.

FISHWIFE. Today we have no play.

CREATOR. Stand over there. I'll see what I can do.

Whispering between them as they move aside.

FISHWIFE. . . . have no play . . .

CREATOR. If you were to walk down the pier at the present hour you'd see no one, but you'd know they were there. The yellowed lace of dresses snatches round a corner just as you turn your head; somewhere, the pulse of music, but if you strain to hear it, you can't: the tune wanders in and out, above and around the snoring anthem of the wind, and the sound of the waves released and pressed again tight on the starfish and anemone-crowded green-brown concrete of the docks. Let's go down, inside.

Interior below ground.

May we have some voices please? Mostly men.

Hushed din: men's voices, a few women.

A woman's laugh.

Woman's laugh at the other end of the room.

The chime of ice.

Ice against glass.

A piano, something . . . wistful.

Indistinct piano, slightly nightmarish. The sounds aggregate and remain, creating the club atmosphere.

Smoke rises from cheap cigars and inches down the walls as the lights dim to half.

The piano stops. Applause.

The piano begins to vamp.

A strange, dissonant vamp in a minor key. Din of voices ebbs.

Deborah comes onto the stage, dressed as a librarian. She is ugly, old and used, with hang-dog cheeks, triple chin, a navel spread big as a fifty-pence piece in the lumbering ocean of her belly and hair that's been bleached so many times it hangs about her face like a wounded animal.

DEBORAH (*on a hand mike*). Good evening, gentlemen. What is it you said? You're having trouble finding Ulysses? Gravity's Rainbow? City of God? Ah, but you're in the wrong section. Couldn't I help you find something more . . . robust?

CREATOR. She moves in rhythm, the last, faint breath of an enticing dance.

DEBORAH. Let me take you to another section. Here. These shelves are mine. All the books are leather-bound, all are first editions. And I don't allow just anyone to read them.

CREATOR. Chassée . . .

DEBORAH. You will hold my golden card, while others are in crowds at the edge of the shelf and can't get a look in.

CREATOR. She slinks and shifts along the footlights and says:

DEBORAH. Gentlemen, I'll be in the bar till dawn. Let's talk about you.

CREATOR. While up above, in a street not a mile away, a yellow-haired girl in bare feet approaches . . . you. And you.

AGEING PUBLIC SCHOOLBOY. Me?

FISHWIFE. Us?

CREATOR. You.

Exterior acoustic: silent street.

SARAH (*approaching*). Can you tell me how to get to the harbour?

AGEING PUBLIC SCHOOLBOY. The harbour?

SARAH. Am I anywhere near it?

FISHWIFE. The harbour!

AGEING PUBLIC SCHOOLBOY. Why do you want to go to the harbour?

FISHWIFE. It's a long way from here.

SARAH. Do I have to cross the park?

AGEING PUBLIC SCHOOLBOY. Which park is that?

FISHWIFE. You have to go over the bridge.

SARAH. Am I anywhere near the bridge?

FISHWIFE. There's no bridge around here.

CREATOR. Footsteps. Enter a minion of the local constabulary.

Footsteps.

FISHWIFE. Evening, Constable.

AGEING PUBLIC SCHOOLBOY. Fine night for a walk, chuff chuff.

POLICE CONSTABLE. Any trouble here?

FISHWIFE. No trouble here, Sarge.

SARAH. Could you tell me how to get to the harbour?

POLICE CONSTABLE. The harbour!

AGEING PUBLIC SCHOOLBOY. The harbour is shut.

FISHWIFE. The harbour never shuts.

POLICE CONSTABLE. Why are you going to the harbour?

FISHWIFE. I was wondering that and all.

SARAH. Couldn't you please direct me?

POLICE CONSTABLE. First I'd like to know why you're going to the harbour.

SARAH. I'm meeting someone. Thank you. I'll ask someone else.

POLICE CONSTABLE. Wait. Don't run off now. Tell me about this person you're meeting at the harbour.

SARAH. No. The truth of the matter is that I'm not meeting anyone at the harbour. And I'll be going now.

POLICE CONSTABLE. What you're saying is you lied to me.

SARAH. I didn't lie. I said I was meeting someone. It's just an expression.

POLICE CONSTABLE. If you say you're meeting someone and you're not, that's not an expression, it's a lie.

SARAH. It's a lie then. Lying's not against the law, so I'll be on my way.

POLICE CONSTABLE. If you lie to your mother it's not against the law, but if you lie to a police constable it could be construed as suspicious behaviour and warrants looking into. The station's just around the corner. Come visit with me for a while.

SARAH. I'm afraid I'm in a hurry.

POLICE CONSTABLE. I'm afraid you're not.

As they depart.

SARAH. Let go of my arm . . .

AGEING PUBLIC SCHOOLBOY. She's under arrest.

FISHWIFE. I never would have known.

AGEING PUBLIC SCHOOLBOY. They teach them to spot the signs.

FISHWIFE. In police training, they teach them to spot the signs.

AGEING PUBLIC SCHOOLBOY. They have to read a book and do examples.

FISHWIFE. Before they give them their uniform.

AGEING PUBLIC SCHOOLBOY. I knew there was something. I could smell it.

His voice fades on this line, cut off by the shutting of a cell door, miked from the inside.

SERGEANT (*inside the cell with her*). Sit down on the bed.

SARAH. I'd prefer to stand.

SERGEANT. I insist.

She sits.

They tell me you were on your way to the harbour.

SARAH. It's not illegal to go to the harbour.

SERGEANT (*a sigh*). May I tell you something, Miss . . .

SARAH. Sarah.

SERGEANT. I'm not interested in disguising my intentions. I'd like to hear your story and put you on your doorstep so I can make myself a cup of coffee and relax with the Sunday Sport. Tell me why you were going to the harbour.

SARAH. To get away from home.

SERGEANT. From the home of Claire St Quentin-Latham? Surely you can see how it looks to us. The St Quentin-Lathams are a pillar of society, well bred, just serious enough, elegant at parties, at home in polite company, and with a dry, ironic sense of humour that never fails to amuse. What could possibly possess you to leave a household of such esteem?

SARAH. They treat me poorly.

SERGEANT. In what way?

SARAH. They have me work eighteen hours a day, seven days a week. I have to take a toothpick to the corners of every room. I have to comb the velvet curtains with a goat's-hair brush. I have to set the portraits in an even line with gravity using a draughtsman's level. They feed me with scraps of food left at the table which they drop into a pot of boiling water, add lard and coarse flour, and bake, creating a doughy mush not unlike slop. When I cook for them they do a biopsy on the flesh of my tongue to make sure I haven't tasted any of their food. They slap me when their hands itch, spit on me when there's too much salt in their food, and when I talk back they hang me upside-down from the chandelier with lead weights tied in my hair.

Pause.

SERGEANT. Do you understand the laws against perjury?

SARAH. Every word I've said is true.

SERGEANT. I don't like liars. If it were not your mother's wish that you be brought home immediately, I'd do everything in my power to make you feel the full muscle of my disgust. But . . . Sarah . . . why the harbour? Were you going there looking for work?

Pause.

For work, Sarah?

Pause.

Stand up.

Keys in lock, door slams, echoes, fades into objective acoustic.

CREATOR. Now just to remind you that there are, in fact, civilised people somewhere in this world, I'll take you to a house at the edge of town, giant, elegant and cold, on a thousand acres of slopes and browning trees. Inside, furnishings are scarce and the rooms uncluttered; chilly, almost, even in summer. A straight-backed velvet settee rises primly out of an oriental rug, Turkish, let's say, and on it a girl does needlework, her legs cast daintily to one side like scarves. A crystal clock ticks like an icicle on the mantle.

Clock ticking.

Music, I think, as well. Mahler's fourth.

Music.

Louise comes in, twisting a daffodil around her finger.

LOUISE. They found her.

ADELAIDE. Did they? Where?

LOUISE. She was on her way to the harbour.

ADELAIDE. Good God.

LOUISE. Mother's waiting in the study.

ADELAIDE. She's not going to like this.

LOUISE. I should say not. Bringing the police into it. Making it public.

ADELAIDE. Some spice to the evening, in any case.

LOUISE. I daresay, thank Heaven above. I'm so bored lately, so bored . . .

ADELAIDE. If I didn't have my needlework I wouldn't know what to do with myself.

LOUISE. Yes, but *I* can't do that. *You* do *that.*

ADELAIDE. You must find something ASAP. Yesterday you lit one match after the other and watched them burn. I saw you in the dining room dropping them into the ashtray. You did it for a full fifteen minutes.

LOUISE. Fire; yes, it does wake one up. A bit of danger, however minute. Sometimes I feel sleepy all day long. Other times I sit down to read and I find myself staring. I don't remember the beginning of the stare. I just realise that I have been staring for some time without knowing it. I look at the clock and it's two hours later. Once I found the gardener watching me through the window. I had to shut the curtains.

ADELAIDE. They're always looking in. They trim the plants nearest he windows for uncanny lengths of time.

LOUISE. Once he passed by my bedroom window. He looked in.

ADELAIDE. He was hoping you were naked.

LOUISE. Why is it they hope that?

ADELAIDE. One would think they'd have something better to hope for, like Christian good in all men or fine weather.

LOUISE. I don't believe they think that way. They work in the day, in the evening they drink, and before sleeping I've heard they want a woman. Without wanting a child, they want a woman.

ADELAIDE. It's so common it makes the hair stand up at the back of my neck.

LOUISE. Their skin is like sandpaper, I've no doubt in my mind.

ADELAIDE. They're like . . . trees that move. It is therefore not within my abilities to comprehend, how on earth Sarah could bring herself to . . . to *touch* . . .

LOUISE. To *hold* . . .

ADELAIDE. To – to – to –

LOUISE. Well, let us say it:

ADELAIDE. To . . .

LOUISE. Do –

ADELAIDE. Such a thing. Beyond my comprehension.

LOUISE. She's a peasant girl. Her blood is a different colour.

ADELAIDE. Her hands were calloused at birth. Still, how she could –

LOUISE. Take –

ADELAIDE. Well, let us say it:

LOUISE. Have –

ADELAIDE. That – that – that –

LOUISE. *Labourer* . . .

ADELAIDE. Is beyond me, quite beyond me.

LOUISE. Mother must have done father.

ADELAIDE. Only for the purposes of perpetuating the species. She wanted to have two little girls and name them Louise and Adelaide. She was married for the love of her two little girls, she was kind to him for the love of her two little girls, she . . . *did* . . . him . . . for the love of her two little girls.

LOUISE. Mother says he was refined, special.

ADELAIDE. He didn't request her more than necessary. Two requests, only two: one for me, and one for you.

LOUISE. Ha! You rhymed! Now I get to spit in your soup!

ADELAIDE. You'll rhyme before supper tomorrow, I have every faith.

LOUISE (*coy*). Mayyybe. Maybe not. Winter's cold, and summer's –

ADELAIDE. Yes?

LOUISE. Rather warm.

LOUISE *laughs, snorting.*

ADELAIDE (*chilly laugh*). Oh Louise . . .

LOUISE. Hot! Hot! I've said it! See, my darling, I've released you, you've been saved! Give me a kiss.

Loud kiss. LOUISE *applauds ecstatically, laughing.*

Ohhh, see how much *fun* things are! If only we could be alone together in this room always without Sarah nosing around, getting *into* things, talking . . .

ADELAIDE. Speaking . . .

LOUISE. *Say*ing things . . . She always comes out on top when she can talk. She turns things around, twists them, and always wins.

ADELAIDE. She won't win tonight. We'll get her tonight. We'll have her tonight.

Cut music, cut sitting room acoustic, leaving clock ticking in a void. It begins to fade.

CREATOR. No no – keep that. Louder . . . yes.

Ease in interior acoustic, vast factory workshop. Ticking crystallises from echoey to harsh and clear.

Now add to that a mechanical hum . . .

Mechanical hum.

Churning cogs . . .

Churning cogs.

A . . . respirator.

Respirator.

Something metallic and rhythmic, and a whistle, perhaps.

Sounds are added to create a cacophony of factory sounds, extreme and cartoonish.

Yes. That'll do nicely.

FACTORY WORKER. P-4-2-5-X-9!

No response.

P-4-2-5-X-9!

No response. Footsteps running, approaching; panting.

WILLIAM (*breathless*). P-4-2-5-X-9!

FACTORY WORKER. Two-thousand short-run self-adhesive four-ply things!

WILLIAM (*fatigued*). Hark, ho, God praise him that filleth my purse.

CREATOR. He positions himself at a great long runway, and out slides a box.

Box slides out.

He binds it, labels it, initials it, and drops it in a chute.

Sound of box dropping in chute.

And out slides another.

Box slides out.

He binds it, labels it, initials it . . . and drops it in the chute.

Box dropped in chute.

And again.

Box slides out.

And again.

Box slides out.

Now I'll bring in Frank, before we *both* go mad.

Box slides out.

His pelvis precedes him into the workshop, his cigarette rounds the corner, and behold, the rest of him saunters in after.

FRANK (*approaching*). Oi mate. Long weekend, eh?

Box dropped in chute.

You better knock off after this runway. The last ferry leaves at midnight.

WILLIAM. The bell hasn't rung.

FRANK. So?

WILLIAM. I can't leave before the bell.

FRANK. Why not?

WILLIAM. I've already had four warnings.

FRANK. We don't have time to queue up for showers. If we miss the ferry we *lose* a day.

WILLIAM. I must obey their orders. I am a robot. They deal the cards and I must play.

FRANK. Pinch yourself, mate. You're not dead.

WILLIAM *begins to laugh, near hysterics. It subsides. Box dropped in chute.*

They're not as strict with me as they are with you.

WILLIAM. You don't have a job, you have a skip through the woods, a flight through the air!

FRANK. My job they let me take a ten-minute break if I just ask for it.

WILLIAM. I did Runway Three four times and Runway Five twice before dinner. I hunch over my sandwich and look at the clock the way a mouse looks at a cat. Now I've done Runway Two twice, Runway Four three times, and I just got transferred to Runway One eighteen . . . minutes . . . before the bell . . .

Sentence broken by crying. Drops box in chute.

FRANK (*compassionately*). I think you're going crazy.

WILLIAM. I can't stand at the runway anymore. I can't stand at the runway anymore. I can't stand there anymore. No I can't, I can't, I can't.

Box slides out.

FRANK. You've got a long weekend.

WILLIAM. And after that I'm not coming back. No I'm not. I'm not coming back. I want to be outside, look at this place, there are no *windows*! I'm not coming back down here. When the bell rings . . . when the bell rings . . .

FRANK. When the bell rings we're going to get on that boat. Shower at the harbour.

Box slides out.

There are places where a shower is included.

WILLIAM. I know. I lived there.

FRANK. At the harbour?!

WILLIAM. By the wood. There was a girl there. She was tame and robust.

FRANK. The women at the harbour are not tame. Some of them are robust but it costs more to get to know them.

WILLIAM. There's a place I heard the women will kill you if you try to leave without paying.

FRANK. Anne Boleyn's. They're the cheapest for starters but they really rake it in on seconds.

Box dropped down chute.

WILLIAM. I've never been to the harbour.

FRANK. How could you live there without going to the harbour?

WILLIAM. I mean I've . . . been to the *harbour* . . . But I've never been . . . to the *harbour*.

FRANK. Me and Donald went every weekend for three months. By Wednesday each week I was living on white rice and surgical spirit.

Box dropped down chute.

FRANK. Oi mate . . .

WILLIAM. Yeah?

FRANK. Don't touch that box.

The bell rings, drowning out all other sounds. When it stops: sitting room acoustic. Only the ticking remains.

ADELAIDE & LOUISE (*singing*). Too too rough, but oh so clear, she went under three times but who's counting my dear . . .

Pause.

LOUISE. I'm bored of that song.

ADELAIDE. Let's sing another.

LOUISE. No. Let's see who can hold her breath the longest.

ADELAIDE. All right. Ready?

Both inhale. Knock at the door. Both exhale.

CREATOR. Claire comes into the room. She is old, but no stranger to the beautician's knife.

Slam of door.

CLAIRE. Nobody move. Do not interject. Do not comment. Sit upright and glance over only occasionally.

Front door is opened.

POLICE CONSTABLE. Evening, ma'am. Here's the girl.

CLAIRE. Thank you, officer. Your efforts are appreciated. I . . . can't invite you in for a cup of tea, I'm afraid. The hour is . . .

POLICE CONSTABLE. No explanations necessary.

The door is closed.

CLAIRE. Face the wall with your hands behind your back. Don't speak! Turn. Louise, get the rope.

LOUISE's *footsteps going.*

CLAIRE. Well now . . . did you enjoy yourself? What was he like? Is he tall? Olive-skinned? *Black*, perhaps? . . . Does he dance well? Is the skin behind his ear soft on your lips and on your tongue?

SARAH. There is no man.

CLAIRE. Then what was waiting for you at the harbour? You must know what kind of a place it is. Would a healthy, clear-minded girl make her way to the harbour in the middle of the night?

LOUISE's *footsteps returning.*

LOUISE. Here's the rope.

CLAIRE. Give it here. No, Sarah, somehow I imagine not.

SARAH. Please don't tie my wrists . . .

CLAIRE. Louise, if you found yourself at the harbour in the middle of the night, what would you do? Make your answer brief.

LOUISE. I'd approach the nearest young couple, old lady or police officer and ask them the quickest route home.

CLAIRE. Adelaide, what would you do?

ADELAIDE. I'd hail a taxi.

CLAIRE. And if there were no taxis?

ADELAIDE. I'd hide in a subterranean electric cupboard and wait till morning.

CLAIRE. Neither of these is the best answer, but they do make the point, which is that it is quite natural to feel revulsion at the thought of a place like the harbour even in the light of day, but at night it would instil unquantifiable horror in any but the most street-hardened tart! Louise, her hands are tied. Hitch her to the post.

SARAH. *Please* . . .

CLAIRE. And yet our Sarah actually *chose* to go to the harbour, darting round the edge of pools of light in the streets, up back alleys, more like a stray *dog* than a young woman!

LOUISE. She's hitched.

CLAIRE. Good.

SARAH. I'm hungry.

CLAIRE (*laughing*). She's hungry! Tell me, someone, why have we fed her? Is her existence somehow so special that she deserves handouts from everyone whose land she ends up on?

SARAH. You had me brought back here, give me some *food*!

CLAIRE. Quiet, strumpet! Adelaide, we had a cat once at the door, didn't we?

ADELAIDE. Mmmmm . . .

CLAIRE. It just turned up one day, quite expecting to be fed. And we fed it.

ADELAIDE. We did.

CLAIRE. What is this quirk in human nature that compels us to feed strays?

SARAH. I want something to EAT!

CLAIRE. Louise, she's hungry. Go and get her a bowl of milk.

Footsteps receding under:

SARAH. Something HARD! I want FOOD!

ADELAIDE. Miaow . . .

SARAH. If you won't give me something to eat let me GO, I'll get something for myself!

CLAIRE. How? You have no money.

SARAH. I'll manage! If you feed me don't pass it off as charity, I'M A PRISONER AND YOU KNOW IT!

ADELAIDE. Miaow.

Footsteps enter; a bowl of milk set on the floor.

LOUISE. There's your milk. Lap it up.

Sound of lapping.

CLAIRE. Good kitty.

ADELAIDE. Miaow.

LOUISE *and* ADELAIDE *share a chuckle.*

LOUISE. I'll bet she met her man last night. Her tomcat.

ADELAIDE. I'll bet he had her up against a building.

CLAIRE. What would you know about such things?

ADELAIDE. I know what *cats* do. Do you feel like a cat when you're doing it, Sarah? Like some kind of street cat with your skirt up around your neck?

CLAIRE. You talk as though you've seen it a hundred times.

ADELAIDE. No, I haven't seen it.

LOUISE. Adelaide, that's not –

ADELAIDE (*covering*). BUT I'D . . . like to. Sarah, couldn't you do it in front of us just once? For purposes of scientific observation only, of course.

LOUISE *laughs.*

I promise we wouldn't say a word. We'd sit there in respectful silence and turn the lights down so you could pretend it was an alley.

LOUISE *laughs harder.*

LOUISE. Up against a wall . . . between two . . . rubbish bins . . .

ADELAIDE (*laughing as well*). And three-day-old bacon and frozen dinner wrappers . . .

LOUISE. SPAGHETTI ON THEIR HEADS!

The two burst into a roar.

CLAIRE. All right, enough! Adelaide, watch her till two, and Louise, take over after that. Don't fall asleep, we're taking no more chances.

Her footsteps receding, interrupted when she stops.

Oh, and if she continues to complain about hunger, give her a leg of pork. But don't cook it.

Shuts door behind her.

ADELAIDE. There's a good pussy. She drank it all up.

SARAH. Untie this rope. It's burning my wrists. Please!

ADELAIDE. 'Please'! What manners! But don't you know, Sarah, only those who are clean go free.

SARAH. I AM CLEAN!

ADELAIDE. Oh, but I don't mean recently clean. I mean clean for all time.

LOUISE. Not clean this month, or clean since the last fall of rain. *Clean.*

SARAH. Take it off. I promise I won't move.

ADELAIDE. No, you *won't* move. Louise, did you ever go up the hill by where the old shed used to be, the shed mother's husband built for storage?

LOUISE (*playing along with delight*). I haven't been up there for years.

ADELAIDE. Well the shed's not there anymore, but there's a small cleft between three mounds, shaded by trees, near the spring.

LOUISE. *Is* there!

SARAH. Do I have to hear this? SHE KNOWS THE STORY, WHY DO YOU HAVE TO PLAY IT OUT?!

ADELAIDE. I saw them there. That was where they did it, her and that gardener. I hid in the grass where they couldn't see me.

SARAH. THAT'S ENOUGH!

ADELAIDE. They were sitting one on top of the other like they were dancing, but with their legs sticking out behind each other.

SARAH. You know NOTHING ABOUT IT!

ADELAIDE. They were breathing like they'd just finished running and she was biting his throat like she was trying to chew her way through to his back.

LOUISE. How odd!

Titters.

SARAH. And I suppose you just happened to be walking by . . .

ADELAIDE. No, I followed you.

SARAH. So you could watch.

ADELAIDE. I *saw* you. I looked over the mound and I saw your face digging, scraping –

SARAH. YOU WATCHED US!

ADELAIDE. I *saw* you.

SARAH. You told me afterwards you watched the whole thing.

ADELAIDE. I only looked for a moment to confirm my suspicions, and I only saw the one image I described.

SARAH. Are you sure that's all you could describe? Couldn't you describe the image of my knees around his ears?

ADELAIDE. If I'd seen anything like that I'd have called in MI5.

SARAH. You watched us and you don't want Louise to know because she might find out you're TWISTED –

ADELAIDE Shut your mouth.

SARAH. Or that in some way you've BETRAYED HER –

ADELAIDE. Louise, pull the cord in.

Sarah groans.

You are a vile-mouthed pig. What you do is only surpassed in filth by what comes out of your mouth.

SARAH. Go away, Adelaide, get out of my sight. Why don't you go up by where the old shed used to be and see if there's a show on? And if you're so disgusted with yourself for being a woman you can bring a needle with you and embroider yourself shut!

ADELAIDE. Tighter!

Sarah groans.

SARAH. As a ritual, under the yawning sky, in full view of the –

ADELAIDE. Pull it in!

SARAH. CLEFT WHERE I –

ADELAIDE. Tight!

SARAH. Ahhh!

ADELAIDE. Don't give her any slack at all.

Pause.

SARAH. Yes, Louise, pull it in. Come on, tighter, have you no strength? Pull it as tight as it will go, you have my blessing. Because I swear to God one of these days I'm going to have you both for dinner.

ADELAIDE (*her voice breaking, overcoming it with volume*). THESE CONSTANT REFERENCES to hunger are breaking my heart. Louise, keep an eye on her. I'll get her a leg of pork, and a stocking to tie it in with. I'm sick of hearing that voice.

Her footsteps recede.

SARAH. Louise . . .

LOUISE. No.

SARAH (*whisper*). Louise . . .

LOUISE. NO! I WILL NOT LISTEN!

Pause. Clock ticking progressively louder.

SARAH. Untie this rope now or I swear before God and man you will die screaming my name.

LOUISE (*voice quivering*). Miaow . . .

SARAH. I will make it my one ambition. I'll have you if I do nothing else.

LOUISE. Shut up! Bad kitty. Miaow! Mi –

The second syllable is the long wail of a ferry whistle, like a woman's scream. Cut loud clock ticking with end of whistle and add waves splashing against boat, opening acoustic to vast night-sea sky.

WILLIAM. Is that the harbour?

FRANK. Yeah.

WILLIAM. That can't be it.

FRANK. Why?

WILLIAM. Because there's no lights on.

FRANK. All the light's underneath, mate.

WILLIAM. Oh.

FRANK. Should be there in five minutes. Can't you just smell it?

WILLIAM. Hmmm.

FRANK. Don't you want a woman?

WILLIAM. Well –

FRANK. Do you want a woman or not?

WILLIAM. I'm not like you, it's not a *function* for me, I've . . . only ever had one woman . . .

FRANK. Bollocks.

WILLIAM. It's true.

FRANK. I don't believe you.

WILLIAM. *One woman once.*

FRANK. Well we'll fix that tonight. Me I can't go a month; I start getting headaches. And there's plenty of women to choose from at the harbour – they say you can do three a night for over four years and never repeat yourself.

WILLIAM. Those aren't women. They're machines.

FRANK. They're different once you get to know them. I knew a girl three or four times before I found out she could put a sentence together. Then I couldn't shut her up. She told me about her uncle in the police department, about the time she got beat up walking home by the anti-vivisection league, and after a while I had to stop seeing that one because of all the conversation.

Pause.

I'll take you to the place you don't have to buy them drinks. I always go there. You can buy them drinks if you want but it's not obligatory.

Pause.

Three minutes.

With the sounds of the sea, now, the same woman's laugh from the club fades in, echoey, distant, grows in volume, and all sound is then cleanly cut to the atmosphere of the sitting room, with the clock ticking at normal volume in the background, and the immediate rustle of fabric as LOUISE starts awake.

LOUISE. How did you get loose?

SARAH. Don't block my way.

LOUISE. Tell me how you got loose!

SARAH. Are you mad? You untied me yourself.

LOUISE. I was asleep!

SARAH. I told you my wrists were burning. You sat up, walked over to me, and burned the rope with the poker from the fireplace.

LOUISE. Liar! You did it yourself!

SARAH. Which is it? Did you let me go? Or did you fall asleep on the watch?

LOUISE. Wait here. I'm telling mother.

SARAH. I'll be gone when you get back.

LOUISE. Just let me get another bit of rope! If you don't, I'll scream!

SARAH. Mustn't do that. Either way you're at fault, mustn't shout them out of bed as well.

LOUISE (*whimpering*). Please don't hurt me . . .

SARAH. Hurt you! What I could do now would be a graze on your knee, a sliver in your finger, compared to what I have in mind! Once I'm in charge, I'll hook you up in the kitchen to set hot pans on, in the sewing room you'll be my pin cushion. No, you're safe for now; I wouldn't dream of relieving you the suspense.

LOUISE (*breaks down crying*). Sarah. . . .

SARAH. Aww, Louise doesn't have the rope anymore, no more playtime . . .

LOUISE. Sarah . . .

SARAH. No no, no rope can stop those tears, Louise. You've got to cut them off your face with knives.

LOUISE. *Please* . . .

SARAH. I'll make a deal with you. Give me five minutes. Let me walk out of here and give me five minutes before you tell mother I'm gone.

LOUISE. You're blackmailing me.

SARAH. This is not blackmail. This is arbitration.

LOUISE. Two minutes.

SARAH. Five.

LOUISE. Three.

CREATOR. The bracelets, now: the exchange of goods for service. Sarah slips a gold ring from her wrist and pulls her sister's fist through; the shine spills like lotion on her arm. Sarah gives her the second bracelet as well, clasps it on the other arm and the two bands of gold dangling in close proximity rinse together, trembling a glimmer geometrically quadrupled, commanding her sister's eyes to suck them in, exponential light.

SARAH. Five.

A door shuts, cutting to the club atmosphere. Applause. The dissonant vamp. DEBORAH *speaks on a hand-held mike.*

DEBORAH. Good evening. It's morning, but I'll say evening. It'll be a civilised evening, I can tell. I see the faces of gentlemen tonight. Gentlemen, who doff their hats when I pass, who flatter and make respectful propositions. Sir, the grey at your temples bespeaks your gentility, and the creases at your eyes make weak my knees.

A throaty laugh.

Ahh, we *are* lucky to have you. And tonight, just for you, we've got a special treat. We've got Julie, as usual, and Bernadette, and Hanna, and Sandy with us all the way from the Ross Ice Shelf – but guess what we found wandering by the dolmen in the hills of the west coast? Her name is Sarah. She was a shepherdess, and she's wandered in and around those crags utterly alone since she was a girl. I'm sure you'll show her that we have more fun here than on one of her frigid inclines . . . She'll introduce herself just shortly. Sarah, enjoy yourself. These are your friends.

The vamp dissolves into improvisation under general applause, and the din resurfaces.

WILLIAM. I feel like I'm in a sewer up to my neck.

FRANK. Hang about. Those two at the bar just waved.

WILLIAM. A spider and a worm.

FRANK. *Women.*

WILLIAM. Oozing, slithering women . . .

FRANK. Just give it half an hour! You haven't even seen the show yet.

WILLIAM. Show?

FRANK. A woman gets up on stage and reveals herself to us.

WILLIAM. Uncovers her thorax? Exposes her bloodsucker?

FRANK. She doesn't take anything off.

WILLIAM. Doesn't she?

FRANK. No. That's part of the act. Instead she'll reveal herself psychologically. Just wait and see. It's a classy place, I wouldn't lead you astray. And it's a beauty tonight, bird I've never seen before.

WILLIAM. Which?

FRANK. That one – there, by the stage.

WILLIAM. Oh God . . .

FRANK. See? They got a few tasty specimens lounging about, wha'd I tell you?

WILLIAM. I know her . . . Oh God, I know her!

FRANK. Don't go with anyone you know.

WILLIAM. She is the only one, that is the thing, that is it, that is her, she is it! She's the only one I've had, she's the only one there IS, that EXISTS, IT IS HER! What is she here for, why is she here?! She can't be part of this, if she scraped her boot on a kerb these women are what would be left behind!

FRANK. She's nice, yeah.

WILLIAM. Nice?! There is nothing else! Besides *women*, women are the muck under her *nails*, there is no *painting*, there is no *art*, there is no *poetry*, there is no *Shakespeare*, there are no *words*, there is no *sky, there is no life! She is it!*

FRANK. Well . . .

WILLIAM. There was a wood between her land and the garden I tended. I saw here there one morning, *just one morning*, she was clinging – to the trees, she was clinging – to the grass. We spent three hours that were *all history put together! She is all history!* And right now she is *there, ha ha, there is no space between us!*

FRANK. What are you on about?

WILLIAM. Look at her! She doesn't belong here, she's trying to contain her nervousness, her shyness, but I *know* her, I know the way her lips move and her eyebrows, and what I don't know I've *filled in since*, I've *devised* her because those three hours put together were greater than the rest of the hours of my life: I KNOW EVERY FLICKER OF HER CHEEKS!

Beat.

I will have her or I will die trying.

The laugh again. Distant. Heels trot up to SARAH.

DEBORAH. Are you ready?

SARAH. I have five minutes yet.

DEBORAH. I mean do you have something *prepared*?

SARAH. I'll improvise.

DEBORAH. Basil tries to limit improvisation to the more experienced girls.

SARAH. I wouldn't have said shepherdess.

DEBORAH. What?

SARAH. Shepherdess. It's not to my taste.

DEBORAH. So change it. The public imagination is captured in the moment, not in memory as is commonly believed.

SARAH. Thank you.

DEBORAH. Speak indirectly, not directly – there is greater eroticism in the absence of direct sexual reference. Never remove an article of clothing – the fantasy of a body is more alluring than the reality of it. And don't sneeze.

SARAH. I won't.

DEBORAH. I'll be backstage, ready to prompt if you dry up. Break a leg.

Her footsteps receding.

WILLIAM. Look at me.

SARAH. I remember your voice. I don't want to see you.

WILLIAM. I'm behind you. Turn and look at me!

SARAH. Don't ask me that!

WILLIAM. I'm not asking! TURN!

SARAH (*turning, breaking down*). Why did you have to come *now*? I'm going to do this in any case and all you're doing is making it harder!

WILLIAM. I won't see you go up there!

SARAH. You won't because you won't be here! All I want is for the knife to swing both ways. They must feel what I've felt. You won't understand and there's no time to explain but once it's gone full circle I'll be ready for you and NOT BEFORE SO GO!

WILLIAM. When can I see you? Should I have to ask? When can I see you?!

SARAH. Springtime.

WILLIAM. Not springtime, that's impossible, it's not one of the choices!

SARAH. You don't have a choice!

WILLIAM (*quiet and intense*). I could grab you by the waist. I could pull you outside and cover your eyes and take you to a valley ten thousand miles away where there would be *no one* where there would be *nothing else* and you wouldn't know the way *back*!

SARAH. There are people to see to.

WILLIAM. What about *me*? You're pulling my guts out with your fist!

SARAH. We'll both be waiting, you're not the only one who'll be waiting . . .

WILLIAM. BUT YOU'RE THE ONE SAYING NO! If it was a hurricane keeping me back I'd SHOUT IT DOWN, if it was a dragon I'd CUBE IT in an OCEAN OF ITS OWN BLOOD, how can it be YOU, how can YOU be the ONE TO SAY NO?!

SARAH. Because I will do what I have to do and all the while I will know that whatever it feels like for us now *the spring will come and all business will be finished*! Now go and don't let me see you here again!

WILLIAM. Meet me tomorrow, at the place where we met in the grass . . .

SARAH. No.

WILLIAM (*a threat*). I'll be here every night . . .

SARAH. Not *one* night, please, not even tonight!

WILLIAM. I'll go DELIRIOUS with you in my head!

SARAH. Go.

The piano vamp imposes itself.

WILLIAM. Tomorrow, in the grass by where the shed used to be . . .

SARAH (*departing*). I won't be there.

*In a brief pause WILLIAM's sobbing can be heard, but it is soon
drowned in general applause. The din diminishes. Dissonant vamp.
SARAH now speaks on the hand-held mike.*

SARAH. Hello. My name is Sarah. And I am not a shepherdess. I am
not a nurse. I am not a librarian. I am not a secretary, not a painter,
not a cobbler, not a peddler, not a cook. I am not a clown. I am not
a whore.

*The vamp swells and fades, giving way to a breeze in a pastoral
exterior. Footsteps crackling leaves.*

WILLIAM. This is the place we were. This is it. This is the place.
Don't go any farther: her smell is on every tree. Look, patches of
grass are missing where she pulled up clumps in her fist or jerked
her head to the side and chewed it with her eyes shut hard.

FRANK. Sounds a bit dodgy on the ecology.

Leaves crackle under their feet as they roam.

WILLIAM. See that flat spot over there by the stream?

FRANK. Yeah.

WILLIAM. There was a shed there, built by her father when she was a
little girl. He built the shed for storage, but he kept it empty and he'd
come up on warm evenings or during the day and take her with him,
tell her fairy stories, hold her upside-down, whip her with daisies,
and talk about what's at the centre of the earth. When he died he
was burned by his wife and her two daughters, and that evening
termites gobbled the shed till all that was left was the square in the
grass where the shed used to be and one whipping-daisy curled up
dead in the green.

FRANK. William, I . . . how can I say this? You've gone barmy.
Loopy. Round the twist, off the deep end! Come with me. I know
a girl who'll make you forget all about your –

WILLIAM. No. She's coming here.

A gust of wind.

FRANK. It's cold, William. What'll you *do* up here?

WILLIAM. I'll keep myself busy. I'll build a house for us to live in,
where the shed used to be. I'll make the walls of plaited stems and
peach skin and shreds of morning glory, the roof a mop of willow
brushes, and a bed of dandelion dust. Inside I'll weave buttercups
in the walls and in the bowls wedge fireflies for light. For blankets:
sparrows' down stitched with spider webs. For curtains: lambs' wool

dyed with African violets. The floor will be earth sprinkled with poppy seeds and one day in late spring she'll wake up with her belly swollen and orange, pink and blue poppies will be growing between her toes to catch the falling child and wrestle him, giggling, into this world.

FRANK. You're off your nut, mate. I'll be at Anne Boleyn's getting what I came for. If you come to your senses, meet me by dawn.

Leaves crunch as he departs. WILLIAM *begins to crack twigs, otherwise silence.*

CREATOR. Well then?

WILLIAM. Well what?

CREATOR (*privately*). Summon them forth.

WILLIAM. Who?

CREATOR. The birds, the insects, the . . . you know, the creatures of the wood!

WILLIAM. What for?

CREATOR (*through clenched teeth*). To help you build the house.

WILLIAM. No.

CREATOR. 'No'? What do you mean 'no'? You're *meant* to.

WILLIAM. I prefer to do this on my own.

CREATOR. What you prefer and what you've been instructed –

WILLIAM. It has more meaning. (*Unceremoniously.*) I hereby proclaim to the birds, the insects, and all the creatures of the wood that I *forbid* them to assist me in this labour, that every stitch in this house will be sewn by these two hands, and that if they wish to be of assistance, the greatest act of good they could perform would be to stay well clear of me and, if they like, perch and sing.

CREATOR (*arch*). Bugs don't sing.

WILLIAM. Buzz then.

Resumes cracking twigs.

CREATOR (*as punishment*). The slam of a door.

Door slams: interior. Sitting room acoustic, clock ticking.

CLAIRE. Don't slam the door.

ADELAIDE. Mother, I'm brimming with frustration and anger.

CLAIRE. Take it out on cooking.

ADELAIDE. I tried, but it's difficult when you're making broth.

CLAIRE. What has got you this way?

ADELAIDE. I can't find my lavender chemise.

CLAIRE. Did you try the wardrobe?

ADELAIDE. Of course I tried the wardrobe!

CLAIRE. Did you look under the cushions of the settee?

ADELAIDE. What would it be doing there?

CLAIRE. Everything finds its way there eventually.

ADELAIDE (*rummaging*). No, it's not here. Although here's the missing pawn from the chess set, three pairs of gloves, and the Chinese paper doll I lost when I was four.

CLAIRE. Have you tried the chest of drawers?

ADELAIDE. Sarah knows where it is . . . Wherever she is, whoever she's with, she knows, she knows where it is!

Door slams.

CLAIRE. Don't slam the door.

LOUISE (*not aggressive, rather dreamy*). The lace is coming off my black dress.

CLAIRE. Sew it back on.

LOUISE. I can't sew.

CLAIRE. Adelaide can sew.

LOUISE. Not lace on dresses, she sews as art.

CLAIRE. I'm sure she wouldn't mind helping out in a pinch, would you Adelaide. I'm sure you wouldn't –

ADELAIDE. No! I won't sew lace on dresses! I swear that if I ever get my fingers around that girl's neck I will squeeze and squeeze until her eyes bulge out like grapefruits and her teeth play Mozart.

LOUISE. Mother, where is she?

CLAIRE. We'll soon find out. I've got three detectives on it.

LOUISE (*delighting in her own misery*). What if she never comes back? What if that's the last we ever see of her?

CLAIRE. She'll be back. And when she is we'll teach her what it means to cross this family.

ADELAIDE. How? She'll just talk her way out again.

LOUISE. She'll just talk.

ADELAIDE. She'll speak.

LOUISE. Mother, her voice!

CLAIRE. Listen to the pair of you, whimpering like puppies, grown women afraid of a mouse! You must be positive. You must know your own power.

ADELAIDE. All due respect, mother, there are limits. We can't hitch her to the fireplace or she won't be able to clean and cook, unless we find an indestructible lead a hundred yards long or staple her ear with a radar-sensitive –

LOUISE (*frenetic*). Stop it! She'll talk. She'll talk and there's nothing we can do about it!

CLAIRE. Isn't there?

LOUISE. She'll frighten me and that's okay because it's just the way things are, it's just the way they are, things, it's just –

ADELAIDE. Shut up Louise. What do you mean, Mother?

CLAIRE. We could gag her.

ADELAIDE. She'll take the gag off.

CLAIRE. Not if we bind her hands.

ADELAIDE. She needs them free for sewing.

Beat.

CLAIRE. Well then we'll have to slice out her vocal cords and I DON'T want ANY ARGUMENTS about who has to do the sponging up.

LOUISE. I did the sponging up when we neutered the cat!

ADELAIDE. I'm not messing my hands with her blood.

CLAIRE. If we use a dull knife there won't be any blood.

ADELAIDE. Or better yet, use a fork.

CLAIRE. If we open her mouth and pull her head back we can make the cut on the inside so all the blood will drop into her stomach.

ADELAIDE. What a very good idea.

LOUISE. We could *burn* her throat by pouring *boiling plastic* –

CLAIRE. Enough.

LOUISE. Or *hot lava*!

ADELAIDE. We don't have any lava.

CLAIRE. Enough! We'll drug her, pull her head back, and slice the cords at the top and bottom. Then we'll string them tight on a Stradivarius and she can play Bach at parties.

ADELAIDE *laughs drily and* CLAIRE *joins in.*

LOUISE. We've got to find her first.

CLAIRE. We'll find her. I give it . . . three days.

Ticking swells and gives way to jazz improvisation in the club.

CREATOR. Seven weeks later and still no joy. The detectives Claire had hired did find her within three days . . . and they found her there at least twice a week since. Her clientele was already at a healthy peak, and there was no shortage of takers.

Music louder.

POLICE CHIEF. Two brandies, please.

BARMAN. Two brandies.

Sets them on the bar.

POLICE CHIEF. This one's for you.

SARAH. Thank you.

POLICE CHIEF. You're Sarah.

SARAH. How did you know?

POLICE CHIEF. You've been described to me.

SARAH. By whom?

POLICE CHIEF. See those three detectives over there?

SARAH. Yes . . .

POLICE CHIEF. I'm their chief.

SARAH. What have they said about me?

POLICE CHIEF. The tall one?

SARAH. Yeah . . .

POLICE CHIEF. He said you're approachable, reticent, arousing, melancholy, fey, spontaneous, provocative, elusive, enigmatic, lateral, demure, articulate and curt.

SARAH. Did he.

POLICE CHIEF. And the short one . . .

SARAH. Uh huh . . .

POLICE CHIEF. . . . . said you play a mean game of trumps, you know the moons of all the planets, can quote esoteric proverbs, scale fish, swim underwater without coming up for air, and flip an egg onto a grill so that when it lands it breaks up, spelling out a quote from Baudelaire in French.

SARAH. And the fat one?

POLICE CHIEF. He said he gave up smoking, alcohol, clean socks, and sold his daughter into white slavery to buy you flowers, tea, a Fiat, a wig, a book on Crete, earrings made of beetles from the Amazon, perfume from the pheromones of bats, three pairs of tights, a live silkworm, a famous monument in France, and a voucher for a pedicure.

SARAH *laughs*.

But there's one thing they all say about you.

SARAH. What's that?

POLICE CHIEF. That you never let them touch you.

SARAH. Nobody touches me.

POLICE CHIEF. I see.

SARAH. And their descriptions say more about themselves than they do about me.

POLICE CHIEF. Do they?

SARAH. Could I change you by describing you?

POLICE CHIEF. I'm willing to let you try.

SARAH. All right then. I'll wager that you won't become my description of you.

POLICE CHIEF. What do I get if I win?

SARAH. I'll buy you another brandy.

POLICE CHIEF. And if I lose?

SARAH. You have to perform an act of my choosing.

POLICE CHIEF. All right.

SARAH. Whatever it is.

POLICE CHIEF. You're on.

SARAH. All right. You live alone. You're a Gemini. Your favourite colour is red, and your one big dream, the dream you've never told anyone about, is that you'd love to set fire to a house and watch it burn.

He laughs.

POLICE CHIEF. Is that it?

SARAH. Mmmmm . . .

POLICE CHIEF. Well I'm afraid you win. I live with my wife. I'm a Libra. My favourite colour is green, and I no more feel like burning a house down now than I did five minutes ago.

SARAH. You see? People's impressions of you often say more about them than they do about you.

POLICE CHIEF. Touché. Now, what is this act you'd like me to perform?

SARAH. I'd like you to burn down a house.

He laughs.

There's more as well. Come with me – I'll tell you a story.

Music gives way to clock ticking in sitting room. The sound of a match being struck.

CLAIRE. Louise, stop lighting matches, it's an ugly habit.

LOUISE (*distracted*). Look how it makes them black. How it sucks all the food out of the wood and leaves only the useless dead black behind.

ADELAIDE. Do as mother says. There isn't a match within a hundred miles you haven't lit.

LOUISE. They're black now. You can't burn what's been burnt, can you, that's what they mean by fighting fire with fire.

CLAIRE. Enough. Fascination leads to obsession, and obsession to madness . . .

ADELAIDE. . . . and mad girls don't get any pudding.

CLAIRE. Correct.

LOUISE. Look at the pattern they make in the ashtray. Remember playing twigs as children? Dropping a handful and trying to pick them up one by one with a stick? I always lost.

ADELAIDE. Mother . . .

LOUISE. Except once, when I cheated, but that was –

ADELAIDE. Mother! I smell smoke.

CLAIRE. So do I. Louise, that's quite enough.

ADELAIDE. No, proper smoke. Look, it's coming in under the door!

CLAIRE. Oh dear God, there's a fire.

Sound of a house on fire. LOUISE *begins to sob under this, as it gets louder.*

Get a bucket, a blanket!

ADELAIDE. The fire's too big!

CLAIRE. Ring the fire brigade!

ADELAIDE. The phone is melted!

CLAIRE. Run to a neighbour then, RUN!

ADELAIDE. The flames are at the door!

CLAIRE. Break the window then! Oh, God help me, Louise stop crying!

A window breaks. LOUISE *wails.*

Take off your shoes, don't step on the glass – quickly, quickly!

Sound of siren and approaching fire trucks.

ADELAIDE (*disbelief*). They're coming!

LOUISE (*strangely*). They'll wash us off, they'll wash us all away . . .

CLAIRE (*with grave suspicion*). How did they know so soon?

The trucks pull up outside, the engines stop, the sirens wind down. Sound of men shouting outside, then water against the house, under the following:

ADELAIDE. Mother, the window, you go out first!

CLAIRE. No. Let them find us in here.

ADELAIDE. It's dangerous!

CLAIRE. They must find us in here.

LOUISE. The hoses, are the hoses coming through the window, are the hoses coming –

CLAIRE. Louise, get hold of yourself, for God's sake!

LOUISE *starts to cry again.*

LOUISE. Adelaide . . .

ADELAIDE (*sitting next to her*). There Louise, quiet now, there's no more danger, it's all gone, all gone . . .

Sound of an axe breaking through the door. LOUISE *whimpers.*

FIREMAN. You all right in there?

CLAIRE. Yes. Come in. The door's open.

Sound of door opening and firemen entering.

FIREMAN. What happened here then? You leave the iron on all night? The cooker? Anybody smoke?

POLICE CHIEF (*entering*). It's all right. I'll handle it.

CLAIRE. Who are you?

POLICE CHIEF. Chief Detective Sean Humphrey. You the lady of the house?

CLAIRE. I am.

POLICE CHIEF. Could you tell me which rooms were affected by the fire?

CLAIRE. Well . . . the study, the library, and the arboretum, rooms used mostly by my late husband. We rarely go in them.

POLICE CHIEF. I see. Is the property insured?

CLAIRE. Of course it is.

POLICE CHIEF. Hmmm. Now . . . correct me if I'm wrong, but in recent years have you taken out a second mortgage on your home and released all servants but the gardeners from your employ?

CLAIRE. Where did you get that information?

POLICE CHIEF. Just answer the question please.

CLAIRE. Well yes, that's true . . .

POLICE CHIEF. Forgive me, ma'am, but you've aroused my suspicions.

CLAIRE. Suspicions!

POLICE CHIEF. A woman living with two daughters, husband dead, the interest on her savings dwindles with each passing day, and in a last ditch effort to get her hands on some cash to maintain the lifestyle to which she's become accustomed, sets fire to the most dispensible wing of the house in order to collect a plump sum from insurance and keep her creditors at bay. Tidy.

CLAIRE. Now surely you don't think we started it on purpose!

POLICE CHIEF. Look there: that lamp is not switched off at the mains.

CLAIRE. Well we . . . forgot, we forget things, it's not a crime to forget . . .

POLICE CHIEF. What are those in the ashtray?

CLAIRE. Those are . . . well those are matches, but that proves nothing, my daughter burns matches for pleasure.

LOUISE. Don't hurt me . . .

POLICE CHIEF. For pleasure? Or were you selecting your weapon, the way a golfer chooses a club?

CLAIRE. This is absurd, we wouldn't start a fire here, this is our home!

POLICE CHIEF. Is it?

Casually.

I'm afraid I have no alternative but to arrest you now and keep you in a dark wet cell with no chance of bail until such time as a forensic investigation can be carried out to determine the cause of the fire.

CLAIRE *begins to sob.*

LOUISE. Mother . . .

CLAIRE. Please . . . please don't take me to prison, I've done nothing wrong, I have a family, obligations, I'm an older woman!

POLICE CHIEF. You'll be released as soon as the investigation is carried out. But I wouldn't hold my breath. The forensics team are in Calcutta teaching monkeys to speak.

CLAIRE. How long will they be gone?

POLICE CHIEF. Till a baboon sings 'God Save The Queen'. Let's go.

CLAIRE (*being dragged away*). Help me, girls! Don't let them take me away! We will avenge ourselves, we know who's done this and we will have satisfaction, we will have blood!

The door is slammed.

LOUISE (*beginning to sob again*). They've taken mother, they'll take you, they'll take me, she's winning!

ADELAIDE. Quiet. We'll go to the harbour ourselves. We'll find Sarah . . . and we'll bargain for mother's release.

LOUISE. She'll drink our blood . . .

ADELAIDE. If she won't be bargained with, we'll carve our name in her cheek.

LOUISE. We can't find her, she'll disappear into the walls and only fangs will be left, to bite, to bite –

ADELAIDE. Gather your strength, Louise. I need your help!

LOUISE. I'm trying mother . . .

ADELAIDE. I am not mother, look at my face!

LOUISE. I'm . . . looking . . .

ADELAIDE. What do you see?

LOUISE. A pretty girl . . .

ADELAIDE. Do you see mother?

LOUISE. No! The prettiest girl, not an old woman.

With meaning.

Never an old woman.

ADELAIDE. Yes, one day . . .

LOUISE. No, never an old woman. There isn't the time. She's got blond hair and fingers that choke. Ha ha! Nothing to laugh at. When I'm a ghost I'll stand by you and you'll feel the chill . . .

ADELAIDE. Pretty Louise, we'll be old together, you know we will. We'll sit together on mother's grave and sing while Sarah rinses our skirts. Touch my hair.

LOUISE. She'll come in . . .

ADELAIDE. There's nobody here anymore. Touch my hair.

LOUISE. Soft . . .

ADELAIDE. Now I'll kiss your lips . . .

LOUISE. She'll come in!

ADELAIDE. Shhhh . . . No one can come in.

LOUISE. She'll . . . she'll . . .

Whimpers, then near-screams.

ADELAIDE. What is it?

LOUISE. It . . . burns!

ADELAIDE. What?

LOUISE. My . . . my . . . wrist, the bracelets!

ADELAIDE. They don't burn, my darling, they don't –

LOUISE. Burn! They burn!

ADELAIDE. They're bracelets, they can't harm you.

LOUISE. They can, they do! They burn. *She* gave them to me and they burn.

ADELAIDE. They don't burn *my* hand. Let me pull them off.

LOUISE. They don't come off, that's the trick, only she can take them off. Why didn't I know?

ADELAIDE. Enough of this, Louise, pull them off!

LOUISE. Fire and fire together, all the fire from the middle of the earth in these . . . two . . .

ADELAIDE. Off! Pull them off!

LOUISE. They don't come off!

Then quietly.

I can't take them off. I need them to pull the breath into my lungs and the blood through my arms . . . I need them for the food to go down and the heart to pump and the eyes to see and the feet to walk BUT THEY'RE LIKE WEARING HELL AND SHE'S GOING TO WIN!

ADELAIDE. Louise, I need you, come to your senses or mother will *rot* in that prison, she will ROT!

She slaps her face.

LOUISE. That hurt!

ADELAIDE. I'm sorry.

LOUISE. No, carry on just like everyone else, there's nothing anymore anyway so slap, slap away!

Begins to cry again, muted.

ADELAIDE. Here. Sit. There. Louise. Breathe. Yes. Good. Air. Good. Quiet. See? Only ticking. Hear the ticking? Good ticking. Calm. Always the same. One tick after the other. Hear it? Pretty tick. We will find her. We will take her. We will have her blood.

The ticking louder, echoey, disproportionate, insane, the snap of a branch cuts it off.

Exterior by where the old shed used to be. The crackling of leaves.

FRANK. Hello mate. All right?

WILLIAM. Take off your shoes. I've cut a half inch off the top of each blade of grass to make them softer for her feet.

FRANK. Oh. Well I won't be stopping. I was just at the harbour and I thought I'd bring you your wages.

WILLIAM. Keep them.

FRANK. No, they're yours.

WILLIAM. You can't spend any money up here.

FRANK. No, I guess not. Ta.

Pause.

Nice house.

Pause.

Donald got the sack for skiving.

WILLIAM. Did he? Could you just – can I get that – there, under your foot . . .

Rustle.

Thanks.

FRANK. Yeah well I guess I better be going.

WILLIAM. All right. All the best.

Beat.

FRANK. You don't care about real things anymore, do you?

WILLIAM. Real things.

FRANK. Yeah, you know, pool and lager and and and bacon sandwiches . . .

WILLIAM. Real things.

FRANK. No, I guess not.

Pause.

All the best.

WILLIAM. All the best.

FRANK's *footsteps approach mike.*

FRANK. Excuse me . . .

CREATOR (*annoyed*). What is it.

FRANK. Can you help him out?

CREATOR. What's the problem.

FRANK. Well he's gone a bit funny, hasn't he?

CREATOR. I like it. I think it works.

FRANK. Yeah but don't you think it could work too if he was . . .
you know, ate bacon still?

CREATOR. Why should he eat bacon?

FRANK. Yeah but it's a *symptom*. He's lost weight, he's got bags
under his eyes hanging down to his knees, doesn't he sleep?

CREATOR. He sleeps.

FRANK. And all this airy fairy talk, what did you *do* to him?

CREATOR. Can we address this later?

FRANK. Yeah, why should *you* care? You can make it all turn out
like you want.

CREATOR. I don't do it out of malice –

FRANK. See a good mate kill himself, that's what you'd like.

CREATOR. Wait for me at the side.

FRANK. Well there are those above you, that's all I'll say.

CREATOR. Is that a threat?

FRANK. That's all I'll say.

CREATOR. I think you'd better leave this minute.

FRANK. And if I don't?

CREATOR. I'll be forced to do something I dislike.

FRANK. Ooooooh, I'm scared. Don't you see me quivering? There
are those above you, you don't have the final say.

CREATOR. Get out!

FRANK. You have been warned!

*Crackling of leaves cut off by applause, heard from a room off main
house of the club, then improvised piano.*

SARAH (*laying down a card*). Seven of hearts.

MINISTER (*same*). Three of hearts.

SARAH. Jack of hearts.

MINISTER. Jack of spades.

SARAH. Queen of Clubs.

MINISTER. Well done.

SARAH. Thank you.

MINISTER. Make your request. But it must be an act I can perform in this room. You've won the hand, but not the game.

SARAH. Stand up on your chair and whistle.

MINISTER. Is that all you want me to do?

SARAH. For the moment.

MINISTER. All right then.

Stands up on his chair and whistles. Descends, sits.

There.

SARAH. Thank you.

MINISTER. Amused you, did I?

SARAH. A great deal.

MINISTER. Your go.

Sound of cards being shuffled, then dealt.

Ace of clubs.

SARAH. Two of clubs.

MINISTER. Two of hearts.

SARAH. Two of spades.

MINISTER. King of spades.

SARAH. Four of spades.

MINISTER. King of Diamonds.

SARAH. Congratulations.

MINISTER. Thank you.

SARAH. What shall I do?

MINISTER. Well . . .

SARAH. You are aware of the restrictions.

MINISTER. Yes.

SARAH. Well?

MINISTER. Kiss the back of your own hand, looking at me.

She does.

Mmmmm . . .

SARAH. Is that all you want me to do?

MINISTER. Yes.

SARAH. Your go then.

Cards shuffled, then dealt.

Seven of diamonds.

MINISTER. Four of diamonds.

SARAH. Four of spades.

MINISTER. Jack of spades.

SARAH (*with finality*). Queen of Hearts.

MINISTER. Well that's it then.

SARAH. It is, your . . . your what? What is it they call you?

MINISTER. Sir. Make your request.

SARAH. There is a house, a property on the road that leads to the
bluffs. I'd like you to repossess the house, evict the tenants, and put
the house up for sale by public auction.

MINISTER. That's quite a request.

SARAH. Is it? Let me tell you a story.

*The slam of a prison gate. Keys turned in a lock. Footsteps descending
stone steps in an echoey passageway. They reach level.*

GUARD. That's it there, on the right.

ADELAIDE. Thank you.

Footsteps proceed. Singing in the distance.

CLAIRE (*singing*) . . . too too rough, but oh so clear, she went under
three times but who's counting my dear . . .

ADELAIDE. Mother?

LOUISE. Mother, it's Louise.

CLAIRE. My babies, have they got you in here too?

ADELAIDE. They let us in to see you.

CLAIRE. Did they? What do I look like?

LOUISE. We can't see you, mother. It's too dark.

CLAIRE. Then why did they let you in?

ADELAIDE. We've brought you some cinnamon biscuits.

CLAIRE. Take them and run! They'll have you in here. It takes three keys to get you out, and one of them hangs lower than the belt!

ADELAIDE. Do you think they'd lend us a candle?

CLAIRE (*laughing*). There's nothing to see.

LOUISE. Us, mother, us!

ADELAIDE. Your visitors.

CLAIRE. He comes only once a night.

ADELAIDE. Who?

LOUISE. Who comes?

CLAIRE. His neck is sweat and his breath sniffs my ear. Oh, my dears, it would be useless to hide because he knows the geography of the room.

ADELAIDE. Who is he?

CLAIRE. He's young, and he's learning the perks of the trade. He rises and falls, rises and falls, like a machine digging for oil. He's the son I never had.

LOUISE (*vacant*). That's good.

CLAIRE (*singing*). Vita brevis, vita brevis, if she floats, burn her, if she drowns, make a cross of twigs . . .

Beat.

Oh, I am truly happy, my darlings. They give me towels to wrap round my knees for crawling, and when they dim the lights the rats do a jig! The accommodation is first rate, and there is heaven in a crack in the wall. Do they have a brochure?

LOUISE. Mother, you're frightening me.

CLAIRE. DO THEY HAVE A BROCHURE?! No, you wouldn't know, you merciless hag! Scratch my leg, quick!

LOUISE. I can't reach!

ADELAIDE. Stop it, you're upsetting her.

LOUISE. Me?!

ADELAIDE. Quiet. Mother, we've been evicted.

CLAIRE *laughs*.

They've locked us out and boarded up the windows. The property's for sale.

CLAIRE. Well I'm not in the market at the moment.

ADELAIDE. We've been looking for Sarah ourselves.

CLAIRE. At the harbour?

ADELAIDE. Every night, all night. We haven't had much luck yet, but when we find we'll hold her hostage naked in a barrel of pins until she agrees to have you released. Oh, and we'll bring you her vocal cords first thing.

CLAIRE. When you find her, thank her for her favours.

LOUISE. We'll thank her by making a dress out of her.

CLAIRE. Her teeth will be buttons!

LOUISE. Her hair, a sash!

CLAIRE. And her hands will clasp neatly at the back.

ADELAIDE. I think it will be tonight, mother. We've been given a lead.

CLAIRE (*beginning to sob*). Tell them to set me free girls. Every minute is a year . . .

The sound of keys.

GUARD (*from distance*). Time's up.

Key turned in lock, which echoes hugely; echo dissolves into exterior.

CREATOR. On the eve of the first day of spring, William sprinkles mustard seed on the cottage path. He bathes and washes his clothes in the stream and cuts off a winter's growth of beard. He knows the day has come: the gentle warmth of the sleepy blue dusk, trees dripping with fruit . . .

Footsteps approaching.

. . . the lilt and sway of the flora and fauna all conspire to create the perfect backdrop for –

FRANK. Hey.

CREATOR. I beg your –

FRANK. No, you listen to me.

CREATOR. Oh, very funny, where did you get that gun, bribe somebody in the props department, who let you –

FRANK. Shut up.

CREATOR. How dare you speak –

FRANK. I'm serious! One more word comes out of your mouth and your brains are part of that tree.

CREATOR. Well now really Frank –

FRANK. 'Well now really Frank', ha! Look who has the last laugh now! You know you're really corny? Yeah, you are, anyone ever told you that? 'Sleepy blue dusk', where'd you pick that up, it's a load of CRAP! You and your fancy language, well *I'm* taking over now, so leg it or watch your kneecaps fly like boomerangs to the South Pole.

CREATOR. Frank, I think you need some professional –

FRANK. What? Professional what?

CREATOR. Now calm down, this is not a criticism, it's just –

FRANK. Professional what?

CREATOR. *Help*, I'm sorry Frank, I think you need some –

The gun is fired. Creator drops, moans, dies.

FRANK. Now piss off ya stupid cow.

He goes up to mike, taps it, blows on it.

Is this on?

Clears his throat. Into mike:

Yeah so like now William gets out of the water, puts on his clothes, forgets about Sarah, and goes with Frank to Anne Boleyn's where they stay for six weeks, living like kings, and their money never runs out.

Sloshing of water as WILLIAM *comes out of river.*

WILLIAM. Frank!

FRANK. Come on, mate, get your clothes on.

WILLIAM. They're wet.

FRANK (*into mike*). His clothes are no longer wet. (*To* WILLIAM.) Now they're dry.

WILLIAM. No they're not. They're soaking wet.

FRANK (*into mike*). The clothes are now bone dry.

WILLIAM. You can't dry them by *saying* that. Look. They're dripping.

FRANK. Well how the hell did *she* do it then?

WILLIAM. She couldn't *change* anything. She sets things up, but after that they move on their own.

Beat.

FRANK. Oh well that's beautiful, that's just beautiful.

WILLIAM. You can *describe* . . .

FRANK. I don't want to describe, I want to control!

WILLIAM. Sorry about that Frank. I'll be in the sun, over there by the tree. When my clothes are dry I'm going to Sarah. That's what's happening, Frank. I really am very sorry.

WILLIAM *pads away.*

FRANK. Shit!

Hits mike.

Shit! Shit! Shit!

Pause.

Well . . . (*Clears throat. Deflated.*) Yeah well so like . . . William's had a wash and he . . . dries himself in the sun, where all the birds are chirping like . . . birds.

Clears throat.

The house is finished, and the smell of the flowers is . . . pretty.

Harrumphs.

By now the . . . autumn clouds have been . . . soaked up in the sea, chased . . . *dashed* . . . (*Quickly.*) dashed from the sky by the spring which, in one sweeping, balletic whirl, breasts out across the blue and wafts down, full and warm, to caress the young . . . wriggling . . . fresh . . . pink . . . earth.

A satisfied giggle.

And tonight's the night sort of thing. It's all sewn up – you know what I mean?

A note of music plunges us into the club, but again we are in a room off the main house.

DEBORAH. Somebody left you a note. It was with the hostess.

Rustle of note.

SARAH. Thank you.

DEBORAH. They don't leave notes for me anymore. I haven't had a note in twelve years. What does it say?

WILLIAM (*echo*). Our time has come. Meet me tonight behind the Fish and Tackle.

SARAH. I've got to go. Will you cover for me?

DEBORAH. What, you – Sarah, you can't go *now*, you're on in a minute . . .

SARAH. No. I'm not.

Beat.

DEBORAH. Well if you walk out now you know who Basil's gonna yell at, don't you, me! Okay, just do a short one tonight.

SARAH. I have to go *now*.

DEBORAH. All right, walk out, but he won't take you back you know. (*Sigh.*) I'll cover. You been good for this place, he'll piss himself when he finds out you've gone. Here, take this for luck.

SARAH. What is it?

DEBORAH. It's a bit of wood from Christ's cross. They say if you're in trouble, rub it and Christ will appear.

SARAH. Does it work?

DEBORAH. Well he didn't appear when I rubbed it but I don't think I was doing it right.

SARAH. Thank you. I'll remember you.

Door is shut.

Exterior acoustic with wind. SARAH's *footsteps echo along the planks.*

SARAH. William?! William, where are you?

She turns onto a gangway with a different acoustic: no longer shielded from the wind on one side, the planks still hollower beneath her feet. Waves heard now as well, not too near, below. Her footsteps slow down.

William? William, are you there?

ADELAIDE. Hold it there, kittycat.

LOUISE. Miaow!

ADELAIDE. There's no tom here.

LOUISE. No tom here!

ADELAIDE. Did you get our note? We knew you'd take the bait.

LOUISE. You're going to get your cords ripped out of your throat now you evil-minded slut and when we get home we're going to use them for elasticating knickers!

ADELAIDE. Open the bag, Louise.

SARAH. I'm turning around now and walking away.

ADELAIDE. What a very good idea, why don't you turn and go? But there's just one question I'd like to ask you before you leave: Do you like the smell of *chloroform*?!

LOUISE *shrieks, giggles and applauds.*

SARAH. What are you doing, get that out of my face!

LOUISE. It's not working!

ADELAIDE (*sniffs*). Bugger. This is Harpic.

SARAH. Don't be foolish, haven't we had enough?

ADELAIDE. Quiet!

A violent slap. SARAH reacts. Under the following the sound of SARAH being gagged and her muted attempts at protest.

That's how naive you are, darling. Tit for tat, eh? We do you, you do us, wash our hands and go out to play? Don't you realise revenge breeds revenge, like – what is the bug that mates itself?

LOUISE. Worm.

ADELAIDE. Like the self-perpetuating worm . . . Only the very pious or the very stupid break the chain. Put her in the bag.

LOUISE. Where are we taking her?

ADELAIDE. There's a disused yacht behind that grinning whale.

LOUISE (*labouring*). She weighs a ton.

ADELAIDE. Did you bring the knives?

LOUISE. They're in my purse.

ADELAIDE. Let me jump on to the deck, then you push, I'll pull.

Jumps.

Ready?

LOUISE (*labouring*). Ohhhh, I think she's –

ADELAIDE. Harder.

LOUISE. . . . stuck on a nail, or –

Sound of cloth tearing following by a thud as SARAH drops onto the deck.

ADELAIDE. Just in here. Quick – this is illegal.

Cabin door is shut.

LOUISE. Now, off with her vocal cords!

She laughs merrily.

ADELAIDE. Take her out and tie her hands.

LOUISE (*gay*). Mother taught me how to tie a sailor's knot. Shall I do that one? It seems fitting, doesn't it, *here*. Anchor's aweigh! Tote that barge! Batten down the hatches!

Squeals with delight.

ADELAIDE. Now take off the gag.

Beat.

LOUISE (*terror*). Take it off?

ADELAIDE. Of course. How do you expect me to get to her vocal cords, through her elbow?

LOUISE. But Adelaide –

ADELAIDE. Do it.

Sound of this under:

LOUISE (*singing*) . . . too rough, but oh so clear, she went under three times –

SARAH (*voice bursting out of the gag*). Louise, don't do this!

ADELAIDE. Help me tie her to the map table, quick.

LOUISE. No, she'll . . . she'll *tell* now she's got her voice back . . .

SARAH. Louise . . .

ADELAIDE. You'll be holding her voice in your hand in five minutes! Now sharpen this against that nautical clock, I'll tie her legs.

SARAH. You remember what I've sworn, Louise. Let me go and you won't hear from me again, but sharpen that knife and –

LOUISE. Quiet! Silence.

Immediately followed by the sound of a knife being sharpened.

We're going to make a sharp cut, aren't we, Adelaide.

SARAH. I swear to you as I've sworn before . . .

LOUISE. Very sharp! Permanent.

SARAH. I can take back what I've done, but if you do this now –

LOUISE. There won't be anything left.

SARAH. I WILL DO SOMETHING PERMANENT AS WELL!

LOUISE. No sound. Only quiet, and the sound of the waves.

SARAH. Take off the bracelets.

The knife stops abruptly.

Take them off.

ADELAIDE. Don't *hear* her, get it sharp!

SARAH. Do it. I won't have them on you.

LOUISE (*a wail*). Ahhhhhhwwww!

(*Crying.*) See Adelaide? You see? She knew! It wasn't in my head, I swore to you –

ADELAIDE. Don't listen to her!

SARAH. Do what I said.

LOUISE. YOU KNOW THEY DON'T COME OFF! (*Sobs.*) They're on to burn forever, the hands are too big . . .

ADELAIDE. You got them on!

LOUISE. *She* got them on, *she* did, that's the trick, and now they bite and they burn forever, she's won . . .

ADELAIDE. Come here Louise!

LOUISE. I'll get it off, I'll –

ADELAIDE. Come HERE!

LOUISE. CUT – it off. The knife won't go through metal but . . . my *hand* . . .

ADELAIDE. Louise, PUT THE KNIFE DOWN!

LOUISE. My hand will come off, look:

ADELAIDE. Louise, *NOOOOOOO!*

LOUISE (*pain and relief*). Ahhh . . . See? It comes off.

ADELAIDE (*tears, defeat*). Louise, your hand . . .

LOUISE (*placid*). It came off.

Sounds of hand dropped.

ADELAIDE (*sick*). Oh God . . .

LOUISE. The bracelet slips off easily now. Look: On, off; on, off.

ADELAIDE (*tearful*). I'll get my needle and thread.

LOUISE. I wish getting bracelets on was always this easy.

ADELAIDE. You're bleeding by the gallon!

Sounds of something hard scraping against the floorboards.

LOUISE. Look, they really *do* have one inside!

ADELAIDE. Don't rub your bone against the floor, it might get infected!

LOUISE (*laughing*). You sound like mother!

ADELAIDE. Let me wrap your stump with my brassiere.

LOUISE. No! Mother mother mother, that's all you ever sound like, that's what you've become!

ADELAIDE. Louise . . .

LOUISE. All the *rules* . . . Mother telling us how to eat, mother telling us how to laugh, mother telling us how to walk, remember that? I remember every word! 'When you walk, breathing must be like drinking in warm tea. Oxygen fuels the bloodstream and the joints, so air must be taken into the lungs at least six times per minute. If you decide you'd like to glance at something while walking, do it quickly and cleanly, with an expression either of lazy indifference or of bemused apathy. Let the muscles of the face hang, relaxed but pert, on the front of the skull. When you would like to take a step forward, gather your red blood cells around the hip area and, using the muscle at the front of the thigh, lift the leg off the ground with the foot and lower half of the leg swinging, controlled, from the kneecap. To land the foot on the ground, aim the toes approximately thirty degrees in front of the hip, and thrust the leg forward until contact is made. Redistribute the blood cells to the heart and limbs by quickly jerking the spine into an upright position so that inertia sends them to the head. From there the brain will send them to strategically diverse parts of the body. But above all, when walking, the mind should always be toying dispassionately with thoughts of what may happen at the place that you are walking *to*.'

She drops.

ADELAIDE. Louise!

LOUISE (*verge of death; whispered*). What may happen . . . at the place . . . that I am walking . . . to . . .

Dies.

ADELAIDE. Louise don't do this don't die don't leave me alone! (*Sobs.*) You, *you* did it, where is that knife, I don't care what happens now *you won't see the light of day*!

WILLIAM (*on the pier, distanced*). Sarah?!

SARAH. William I'm here!

ADELAIDE. No you don't you don't talk you don't AHHHH, put this IN it, put this –

Sound of WILLIAM *jumping onto the deck.* SARAH *cries out as best she can, gagged. The door to the cabin is opened.* ADELAIDE *begins to sob.*

WILLIAM. Dear God, what on earth –

ADELAIDE. Take her! Take her, she was ours . . .

WILLIAM. Sarah, who's tied you up?!

ADELAIDE (*defeated*). Let her go, take her away, leave me alone with my sister . . .

SARAH. Untie my arms.

WILLIAM. Who's done this to you?!

ADELAIDE. I did! I did it all! Now *take her away*!

WILLIAM. God in Heaven, what's this?!

ADELAIDE. Give me that hand, GIVE IT TO ME! AT LEAST LEAVE ME SOMETHING!

SARAH. Adelaide –

ADELAIDE. YOU'VE WON! NOW LET ME GO!

Door to the cabin is opened. ADELAIDE's *footsteps trample along the deck and fade in distance.*

WILLIAM. Oh my God my heart, seeing you like this . . .

SARAH. Now untie the left arm, quickly, please! I've got to follow her!

WILLIAM. It's done.

SARAH. Now you go back. Don't stay here. I'll meet you at dawn.

WILLIAM. I'm not leaving you!

SARAH. I give you my word I'll see you at dawn, trust me!

WILLIAM. But I've got you now, you're in my hands . . .

SARAH. You've waited this long. It's almost over. I'll see you at dawn.

Slam of cabin door.

WILLIAM. Sarah! *Saaaaarrraaaaaahhhhh*!

His voice fades on this line.

The wind howls about ADELAIDE, *as we dissolve to an exterior outside the prison door, with* ADELAIDE *just running up to it. She slaps her open hand against the door.*

ADELAIDE. Unlock the door, open it up! Let me in!

The door is opened with a low-pitched squeal. ADELAIDE's *footsteps now in a corridor, then silence but for her breathing. She catches her breath before she speaks.*

Mother, Louise is dead. She cut her hand off with a knife. I've brought it with me. See? No, of course you can't see. Here it is, mother. (*Sobs.*) I can't take anything more. I'm wasted, used up. She's scratched at my insides and there's nothing left to scratch and I'm limp now, mother, and I want you home . . .

Footsteps.

GUARD. Would you like some light?

ADELAIDE. Yes.

A match is struck. ADELAIDE *moans – deep emotion and finality.*

GUARD. She's been hanging there since noon. By law we're not meant to cut her down till the coroner arrives.

ADELAIDE (*quietly*). Do you see this? This is my sister's hand. She was clean, and the hand held flowers . . . It was *with* me, too, it was always soft on me and warm. We were virgins together. There were no men.

GUARD. I'm afraid you'll have to go. Visiting hours are finished.

ADELAIDE. She's standing next to me now. I can feel the chill.

Cut to exterior.

Wind rougher than before.

FRANK. Where the pier hits the shore the bluffs begin, three times as tall as the lighthouse below and stretching rough in the night in and out against the wind as far as you can see, like the hard-staring flat faces of dogs. We're on a slope leading to the verge, with the knee-high grass tonight whipping flat on the hill.

SARAH (*distanced*). Adelaide! *Aaaaaadelaaaaaaide*! (*She approaches.*) Excuse me!

FARMER. Ahoy!

SARAH. Have you seen anyone come this way?

FARMER. Like who?

SARAH. A woman.

FARMER. What sort of woman?

SARAH. Any woman!

FARMER. A madwoman?

SARAH. Is she *mad*?!

FARMER. The one that passed five minutes ago, she had one eye looking at the ground, one at the sky, and six birds flying around her head!

SARAH. Where did she go?

FARMER. Through those trees.

SARAH. Thank you!

FARMER. But if you follow her, be careful! Them's the bluffs down to the sea! I lost a horse there once meself in a high wind!

His voice distances on this line. As SARAH *moves toward the trees.*

SARAH. *Aaaaaaaadelaaaaaaaaide*!

Change of acoustic now: among trees.

Aaaaaaaaaaadelaaaaaaaaaide!

She proceeds and comes out on the other side of the trees: full-force gale now, waves crashing far below.

Adelaide, where are you?

ADELAIDE (*distanced, a snake*).

Sssssssssaaaaaaaarrrrrraaaaaahhhhh . . .

SARAH. I'm here Adelaide!

ADELAIDE (*closer as* SARAH *approaches*).

Sssssssssaaaaaaaarrrrrraaaaaahhhhhh . . .

SARAH. Get away from the edge!

ADELAIDE. Sarah, you mousepot, heavenly angel, watch your sister dance!

SARAH. Come here, grab my hand!

ADELAIDE. It'll pull my fingers off!

SARAH. I can't hear you, come closer!

ADELAIDE. No no, no more tricks, you've won now, finish it off!

SARAH. Adelaide –

ADELAIDE (*singing*) . . . too too rough, but oh so clear . . .

SARAH. I want you to come *with* us!

ADELAIDE. There's nothing left of me . . .

SARAH. Live with us! I *want* you!

ADELAIDE. The way a cat wants a mouse? Ha, you've got blood on your claws!

SARAH. Come with me, I'll serve you every minute of the day!

ADELAIDE. Do you think we can start again?

Breaks down crying.

My sister cut her *hand* off . . .

SARAH. You're in a dangerous place!

ADELAIDE. What's a dangerous place? She's *dead*.

SARAH. GRAB MY HAND, YOU'RE KILLING ME!

ADELAIDE: It's too late, I've got the music in my feet, look! I can move, I don't want to go now, my future's all in front of me, shining like a crow's eye, watch your sister dance!

SARAH. ADELAIDE, NOOOO!

ADELAIDE. Louise is dead and mother can't dance anymore 'cause her feet don't touch the ground, she's up on the wall now, hanging from a peg, a clock's wrinkly ticker, calling out the strokes of twelve!

SARAH. Come over here, DANCE WITH ME!

ADELAIDE. . . . she went under three times . . .

(*Broken by sobs.*) . . . but who's counting my *dead*! (*Last burst of energy.*) You've won, Sarah, I'm dancing for you!

SARAH. YOU'RE KILLING ME!

ADELAIDE. I'm dancing for you, Sarah – I'M DANCING FOR YOU!

The sound of a giant rock cracking.

SARAH. Oh God *NOOOOOOOOOOO!*

ADELAIDE'*s piercing wail as she plummets to the waves and rocks below.*

Oh God no . . .

SARAH *sobs. The gale slowly drowns her out, swelling to unprecedented volume as if in triumph.*

Wind slowly dissolves. Silence. The snap of a twig. Acoustic now more intimate than any previous: inside SARAH'*s head. The following should not be 'delivered' like a monologue, but should be like two minutes of thoughts or like two minutes of a dream – and like thoughts or a dream, images emerge and impose themselves arbitrarily and unexpectedly, hence there should be sharp edits where the asterisks are, so that the words either connect or overlap.*

SARAH. To William. Alone now. To William. Alone. Time before I'd done all this. Clean time * soft and clean. Me alone now. Dead dirty alone * ha * William * home. * down and down * stop looking at me! Dawning sun, warming to come home to, soft grass and plaits of flowers of ribbons of rock to make all time string into one vast never-ending sky of * NOW DIRTY * NOW DIRTY * never that way again. My touching will be lying, my kiss will be dry, shhh * no! * slow * stop * slow . . . walk . . . walk. What is that water, the ripple? Saying something. Not to me. It shrinks back from me. Only I can't shrink back. I am it, it is me. Inside it will not ripple but it will not rot, it will stay hard as earth inside and when the days are old and there is a child between us, in his quiet, happy laugh he will not know what's gone past, but he will hold my dirt inside him. Her, in her womb. Us, in our love.

Fade in warm exterior with singing birds. Pause. Then the crack of a twig close to mike. FRANK *chuckles.*

FRANK. She arrives at the house, and what do you know, she kisses him, the *first* lie. There's a wall between them, of glass . . . What do *you* know about *that*? A lot, I'll bet.

A little laugh.

Her eyes don't look at him, weeks click by, she doesn't look at him, funny that, not once, I wonder why? And when she does look at him, there's no question in her face, there's no 'imploring', he has no answer and she knows it, she's alone.

Laughs again, tickled by this thought.

She's more alone than anybody you've ever heard about! Yeah. She'll think sometimes of going away somewhere far where the spring won't smell so RABID but he'll always talk her round, slapping the earth of their house where her father once sat and saying that his good ghost is there to warm her when things get too dark. *Warm* her? Well you know what I say to that? (*Whispers.*) Sarah, can you feel the chill?

Laughs quietly.

So they'll stay in this place, that *was* the *plan*, wasn't it? They'll stay ever after the birds have stopped their music, long after they've stopped seeing each other when they're in the same room, long after even the refuge of each other's necks and smells and arms is not enough anymore they will be here, living out their plan, living their blades of blue grass and their silver-specked river and their sing-songs and their silence and their one hundred thousand nights when the moon, lit up like a dumbstruck nun, passes through the sky quiet – and unseen.

Pause.

And now, then: fade the music.

Baby crying in distance, which fades with acoustic.